ATLA Monograph Series
edited by Dr. Kenneth E. Rowe

1. Ronald L. Grimes. *The Divine Imagination: William Blake's Major Prophetic Visions.* 1972.

2. George D. Kelsey. *Social Ethics Among Southern Baptists, 1917-1969.* 1973.

3. Hilda Adam Kring. *The Harmonists: A Folk-Cultural Approach.* 1973.

4. J. Steven O'Malley. *Pilgrimage of Faith: The Legacy of the Otterbeins.* 1973.

5. Charles Edwin Jones. *Perfectionist Persuasion: The Holiness Movement and American Methodism, 1867-1936.* 1974.

6. Donald E. Byrne, Jr. *No Foot of Land: Folklore of American Methodist Itinerants.* 1975.

7. Milton C. Sernett. *Black Religion and American Evangelicalism: White Protestants, Plantation Missions, and the Flowering of Negro Christianity, 1787-1865.* 1975.

8. Eva Fleischner. *Judaism in German Christian Theology Since 1945: Christianity and Israel Considered in Terms of Mission.* 1975.

9. Walter James Lowe. *Mystery & The Unconscious: A Study on the Thought of Paul Ricoeur.* 1977.

10. Norris Magnuson. *Salvation in the Slums: Evangelical Social Welfare Work, 1865-1920.* 1977

Mystery & The Unconscious

A Study in the Thought of Paul Ricoeur

by

WALTER JAMES LOWE

ATLA Monograph Series, No. 9

The Scarecrow Press, Inc., Metuchen, N.J.
and
The American Theological Library Association
1977

Library of Congress Cataloging in Publication Data

Lowe, Walter James, 1940-
   Mystery & the unconscious.

   (ATLA monograph series ; no. 9)
   Bibliography: p.
   Includes index.
   1. Ricoeur, Paul. 2. Mystery. 3. Subconsciousness.
4. Freud, Sigmund, 1856-1939. 5. Psychoanalysis and
religion. 6. Fallibility. I. Title. II. Series:
American Theological Library Association. ATLA mono-
graph series ; no. 9.
B2430.R554L68   194   76-44865
ISBN 0-8108-0989-3

To my parents

CONTENTS

EDITOR'S NOTE

Since 1972 the American Theological Library Association has undertaken responsibility for a modest dissertation publishing program in the field of religious studies. Our aim in this monograph series is to publish in serviceable format and at reasonable cost two dissertations of quality each year. Titles are selected from studies in the several religious and theological disciplines nominated by graduate school deans or directors of graduate studies. We are pleased to publish Walter Lowe's fine study in the thought of Ricoeur as number nine in our series.

Professor Lowe is a native of Madison, Wisconsin. Following undergraduate studies at DePauw University he studied philosophy at the University of Louvain and Paris. After two years abroad Mr. Lowe returned to Yale University where he completed basic theological studies and the doctorate. He now serves as Assistant Professor of Systematic Theology at Emory University.

A special word of appreciation goes to Professor Julian Hartt of the University of Virginia for his helpful foreword.

Kenneth E. Rowe,
Series Editor

Drew University Library
Madison, New Jersey

FOREWORD

This is an extraordinarily clear, careful and subtle study of fundamental elements in the thought of Paul Ricoeur. Examination of the relationships of mystery and the unconscious--what Lowe properly identifies as a Marcellian formulation--leads inevitably into Ricoeur's treatment of Freud. Lowe's treatment of this famous venture of Ricoeur's is far more than an exposition; it is a critical interpretation of central movements in Freud's thought as well. Here Lowe refuses to follow the route of the liberal theologians who early and late have plumped for revisionist interpretations of Freud calculated to render his doctrines acceptable for their versions of the Christian faith.

The implications of this study for the treatment of theological method are fully as important as the light it throws on Ricoeur and Freud.

Julian N. Hartt,
Kenan Professor of
Religious Studies,
University of Virginia

GENERAL INTRODUCTION

if often he was wrong and, at times, absurd,
to us he is no more a person
now but a whole climate of opinion

under whom we conduct our different lives:
Like weather he can only hinder or help...

--W. H. Auden,
"In Memory of
Sigmund Freud"

GENERAL INTRODUCTION

> When one has all four they will I hope all
> swim in solution like clockwork fish and the
> whole job float like a Calder mobile.   Espérons!

    Thus Lawrence Durrell to Henry Miller regarding the
volumes of The Alexandria Quartet upon which he, Durrell,
was then at work.[1]   For the present study I confess to a
similar ambition.   Such mobile-like complexity seems to me
essential to any reflection of human experience.   The device
may be of simple parts, as this study will be, but it will
want to be intricate in its movements.   The parts are such
as "intellect" and "emotion," "primary and secondary process."
In concluding Parts 1 and 2 and in the General Conclusion I
give them a tap to see if they dance.   Espérons.

a.   five purposes

    But first one must walk, and the reader of any intro-
duction has the right to a statement of purpose.   The present
study responds to several aims which I shall spell out as
straightforwardly as I can, beginning with the most encompassing.

    Primo.   The study's first axion is that theology should
never quite abandon her aspiration of one day seeing all things
clearly and all things whole.   A religious tradition which confesses the incarnation of God, especially, cannot support that
any alleged hierarchy of human experience should relegate
some aspect of that experience to the fosse of the unworthy
or the unredeemed.   This is not to propose that the truths
of other sciences may spring fully clad from the forehead of
theology; but it is to say that theology has a vested interest
in ferreting out points of contact with the languages of other
disciplines.   The delineation of one or two such points of contact is the primary purpose of the present study.

Secundo. A certain concept of "mystery" is well suited to this theological effort. I therefore propose to adopt
Gabriel Marcel's classic distinction between "mystery" and
"problem." A problem is an issue which, in principle at
least, is susceptible of resolution. An instance of mystery
arises within a discipline, but is unsolvable within that disci-
pline--and thus signals a point at which the discipline is con-
stitutionally open-ended.[2] But that is just what is needed in
a point of contact. The delineation of one or two such instances of mystery becomes therefore a secondary, derivative
purpose within the present study.

Tertio. The most honest way to adduce an instance
of mystery is to have wrested it from an unpromising soil.
Thus freudian psychoanalysis is interesting to us by virtue of
its very recalcitrance. For to many minds some version of
psychoanalysis is all the metaphysic that modern experience
allows. So elevated, psychology looms as obstacle and alternative to traditional religious belief.[3] The French commentator Jacques Ellul perceives that the impact of psychoanalysis has been to effect a continental shift in our self-percep-
tions. His reckoning of the human cost of this "school of
suspicion" is negative in the extreme. Ellul gives us a
touchstone which needs to be quoted at length, lest we become too sanguine about just how resistant the freudian soil
may be.

> Everyone knows the paths along which Freud has
> led us, starting with the sick person teaching us,
> on the evidence of the sick person, what it is that
> constitutes the depths of the conscious, willing and
> artificially constructed being. . . . The person is
> such a minor outcropping of the powers dwelling
> within that we have learned not to trust it any long-
> er.

> School of suspicion--that, in fact, is what it all
> comes back to. We have learned no longer to place
> our confidence in anything, no longer to have faith
> in anyone, no longer to believe in a person's word,
> nor in a sentiment, no longer to accept the lasting
> quality of a relationship. . . . We have learned that
> every good feeling merely expresses some self-
> satisfaction or some hypocrisy, that all virtue is
> a lie, that all morality is false, that all devotion
> is vain or a sham, that all speech hides the truth.
> We have learned that only the lie is true, that only
> the murder of one's father is consistent with one's

being, that incest with one's mother is the greatest
desire, that we are never disinterested, that we
are incurably insane for money, whether we have it
or not, for our social class, for our childhood. [4]

Ellul concurs with Auden that "To us he is no more a per-
son/ Now but a whole climate of opinion. . . ." But Auden's
"In Memory of Sigmund Freud" is a tribute; Ellul's passage
is a lament. The problematic of this book is epitomized in
the clash of these two assessments of Freud. [5]

        Religious believers have been similarly divided. Those
siding with Ellul often seek to pull the teeth of Freud's suspicion by charging him with a confusion of realms. They
hold that Freud has arbitrarily collapsed certain distinct
modes of thought, such as "explanation" and "interpretation."
This is the critique set forth by many of Freud's academic
detractors. [6] But if opponent and onlooker alike are unswayed
by this critique, if the "climate of opinion" remains as unaffected as the weather, the reason may not be accidental.
For in its rightful assault upon one vice of our culture,
namely the corrosive reductionism of "suspicion," the distinguishing of modes of thought has unwittingly abetted another contemporary vice, namely the fragmentation of the self.
Conversely, in mounting an explanatory framework which for
all its cosmic sweep maintains a capacity for close, fine-
grained analysis, Freud the alleged reductionist holds out the
promise that fragmentation may yet be overcome. Many will
cheerfully waive certain niceties of distinction in return for
a promise of "identity" and "integration."

        The frustration of this first sort of criticism points
up a difficulty in any approach which assumes, with Ellul,
that Freud is simply a reductionist. Distinction-making is
made to seem mere cavilling by its disinterest in integration.
When theology views psychoanalysis thus--yielding Freud the
body, as it were, and reserving for itself the soul--it tacitly discounts the vital link, the point of contact, which is the
heart of our initial purpose. Worse, it admits that the point
of contact may not be there to be sought; and in so doing it
portrays, it seems to me, a certain failure of nerve.

        Our own purposes, in any case, require another ap-
proach. We must wager that viewing Freud as a flat-out
reductionist is itself reductionistic. Now a way of achieving
this would seem to be offered us ready-made in another common approach to Freud. This alternative would follow Auden
when he speaks of Freud as one of "those who were doing us

some good, / who knew it was never enough but/ hoped to
improve a little by living. " Here, to point up the contrast
with the reductionist, I will speak of a revisionist interpretation. [7] The option seems providentially fitted to the
religionist's needs, for it is inspired by an abhorrence of
certain reductionist tenets. But let us check our gratitude
until we have seen where this alternative leads.

    The revisionist--to sketch a type--will characteris-
tically begin by lamenting the founder's weakness for such
mechanistic metaphors as "drive, " "force, " "repression" and
the like. This misfortune is laid to the prestige of
Helmholtz's physics during the impressionable period of
Freud's early work. Freud was after all the child of his
times. Insofar as the revisionist yet prizes the title of
"freudian, " the resultant determinism is discounted as inessential to the master's position. Or rather it is confined to
the initial stages of human development. For, as Peter
Homans has noted, the distinguishing of stages is a key
move of revisionist theory.

        ... the development of the individual is projected
        as one of initial socialization, in which the self is
        formed in the image of others, and subsequent dis-
        engagement, in which it 'transcends' environmental
        formation and becomes unique. [8]

    To judge from common response, the most stubborn
core of freudian scandal lies not in sexuality, as is often
thought, but in the proposition that life's scenario has been
fatally set, if not played out, by the time we awake from
unwitting infancy. This is a notion which still has capacity
to shock and much of the revisionist doctrine of stages is
formed by rebounding from it. The self is offered the prospect of growth out of determinism into self-determination.
And all the better if the vision be endorsed in the name of
the master himself. Thus an adjunct to the revisionist case
would argue that Freud himself was latterly traveling--again
the stages, now in Freud's own life--or was at any rate
gesturing down, the broad and commodious path which the
revisionists were soon to tread. [9]

    A goodly company of theologians have been prepared
to follow after. To quote Homans again, "the psychological
writings of the third force have been extremely attractive to
pastoral and systematic theologians. "[10] And little wonder,
for the allure of revisionist interpretation is self-evident

when set against the bleakness of the reductionist alternative.
But one wonders whether entente with Freud is really so
easily won. The revisionist's discrimination of stages is a
bit too reminiscent of the academic critic's discrimination
of spheres of discourse, rendered now in chronological guise.
The developmental motif lends a sense of connectedness
which the former tactic lacked, but over-hasty concord in
pursuit of an ill-defined wholeness is little better than
straightforward defection from the integrative task.

    The question thus remains whether the truth of Ellul's
lament has yet been fully addressed. Have we really found
a point of contact within the discipline of psychoanalysis, on
Freud's own terms? Or has the distinguishing of stages at
which Freud is more or less applicable furnished yet another
device for skirting around Freud rather than working through
him? And as for the warrants which the revisionist would
extract from Freud himself, do they bear scrutiny? To
answer these questions--and if need be, to hammer out our
own "third way" between the Scylla of reductionism and the
revisionist Charybdis--will be our study's third and tertiary
purpose.

    Quarto. The influence of the French philosopher Paul
Ricoeur has been with us throughout our enumeration. Those
who are familiar with his work may have sensed that each of
our purposes in some way bears his mark. Yet I have
chosen to spin out the goals deductively, irrespective of
origins, in order to make clear that our "study in the
thought of Paul Ricoeur" finds its rationale within a complex
of larger concerns. We shall study Ricoeur, but we shall
do so in order to gradually lift out an issue which I believe
to be important to any confrontation between theology and
psychoanalysis. It is in this sense that I propose "a study
in the thought of Paul Ricoeur" rather than "a study of."
The distinction does need to be underlined because throughout the body of our study, until the General Conclusion, it
is Ricoeur who will occupy the foreground. Only the way in
which we treat the Ricoeur material will reflect our larger
purposes.

    With this caution duly posted and with recognition paid
the fact that Ricoeur would indeed be deserving of study in
his own right, we may briefly note the points at which his
work meshes with our announced purposes. [11] As regards
the first, the concern for theology and a point of contact,
Ricoeur has made significant contributions to the philosophy

of religion and his writings reflect a remarkably cosmopoli-
tan interest in the relationships between that discipline and a
number of other fields. [12] As regards the second purpose,
treatment of the marcellian concept of mystery, Ricoeur himself recalls "le choc philosophique décisif" provided him by
the thought of Marcel, an inspiration apparent throughout
Ricoeur's detailed meditation on the mystery of the body. [13]

As regards psychoanalysis, the core of Ricoeur's De
l'interprétation is a two hundred and fifty page "Lecture de
Freud" which achieves a fine creative balance between
textual study and reflective generalization. As much as any
philosophic or theological work of which I am aware, the
"Lecture" does manage to work through Freud rather than
dodge around him. [14] Moreover the reader is soon struck
that Ricoeur's exposition of Freud is sufficiently dense and
suggestive to invite a commentary of its own. (In time I
shall argue that the need not only for commentary but for
reformulation is more acute than has yet been recognized.)
Yet of the several studies we now have of Ricoeur, none has
come to grips specifically with the "Lecture. "[15]

For these reasons we may adopt as a fourth purpose,
subordinate to the previous three and as a means of accom-
plishing them, the analysis and reformulation of Ricoeur's
commentary on Freud.

Quinto. That was the extent of my original plan for
the present study: an interpretation of Freud by way of
Ricoeur showing how a certain concept of mystery could be
operative even within the psychoanalyst's program of demys-
tification. But a brief prologue would be needed, a sketch
of Ricoeur's earlier works in which a concept of mystery
had been more or less explicit. His Le volontaire et l'involontaire presented an easy case: it spoke expressly of a
concept of mystery, the concept was apparent in the polarity
of "voluntary" and "involuntary, " and in the book there was
even a forerunner of the "Lecture, " a section on Freud and
the unconscious. [16] L'homme faillible, I saw, might be a
little more difficult. Nevertheless, I knew that a certain
use of polarity was to be my key to an understanding of
mystery, and a polarity was advertised in L'homme faillible's central concepts of the "finite" and "infinite. " The
application of this polarity to the intellect, the will and the
emotions was laid out in the very Table of Contents. [17] By
all indications I could swiftly dispatch L'homme faillible.

And yet I soon realized that, having an eye toward Freud, I read L'homme faillible with certain questions in mind. And I was less and less happy with what I found. My uneasiness centered upon the "finite/infinite" polarity. Was it really adequate to the full range of human experience, as Ricoeur suggests, or was its true home the intellect? And was it extended to the will and emotions solely by courtesy of analogy? The question disturbed me because if anything were to be cast out, it would be the emotions; and within the emotional spectrum from "pleasure" to "happiness," the victim would be the lowly offices of pleasure. To recall our own first purpose, it seemed that tribute was being paid to a certain hierarchy in human experience and that, despite Ricoeur's protestations, even contrary to his intentions, certain "lower" aspects were dropping through the nets of scrutiny. Certainly Ricoeur had brilliantly illumined the structures of emotional experience; like Freud, he had shown that there is a shape and logic even here. But had he shown what within those structures is specific to the emotional life? Granted too, Ricoeur had given some indications about what distinguishes the emotions, but did those indications really fit the "finite/infinite" framework? If it could not receive this, the framework was inadequate after all, and it could not provide footing for a comprehensive notion of mystery.

As I brooded thus, I began to sense beneath my feet, as it were, an other, subterranean framework--one which showed above ground only episodically but which, it increasingly seemed, had shaped the entire landscape of L'homme faillible. If that framework could somehow be unearthed, it might be twice worth the effort: we would gain a model of conscious experience, to eventually compare and contrast with the unconscious; and if the model were to take a certain shape, we would have a first instance of mystery to sharpen that concept before we entered upon the mists of the unconscious. So I began to excavate. The result has added a second full panel to the study, an exposition of "The Structure of Consciousness in L'homme faillible" equal in extent to the treatment of "The Logic of the Unconscious in the 'Lecture de Freud'." The affinities and contrasts within and between these parts are the source of whatever mobile-like quality the study may achieve. But in saying this we run ahead of ourselves. For the moment it is enough to note a reconstruction of L'homme faillible as our final derivative purpose.

b. background

Our sequence of purposes makes clear that while Ricoeur is to be our guide, he is to be such in a specific
sense. Selected issues in his thought--some explicit and
some implicit, some recognized and some unrecognized by
Ricoeur himself--are to provide the occasion for sharpening
an understanding of the human condition, with an eye toward
the way that condition articulates with theology.

First, however, it may be helpful to acknowledge the
larger context in which L'homme faillible and the "Lecture
de Freud" appear. A digest of all Ricoeur's writings would
of course carry us beyond the bounds of the present Introduction. It would be a duplication of effort as well, since
two extensive commentaries are now available and since Ricoeur himself has fashioned summaries of three of his major
works.[18] But a brief interpretative survey might not be re-
dundant if it would stress a few of the concepts important
for an understanding of L'homme faillible and the "Lecture
de Freud." The reader unacquainted with Ricoeur may gain
at least a general sense of Ricoeur's concerns; and others
will be alerted to the particular way we will be approaching
that complex body of thought.

Ricoeur's constructive writing, as distinguished from
his commentaries on Marcel and Jaspers, began with the
vision of a multi-volumed Philosophie de la volonté. But the
coherence of Ricoeur's original vision has been obscured by
the scattered fashion in which his works have found their way
into English, four early pieces being distributed among as
many publishers. So let us begin with a selective bibliography.[19]

A. The original, unfinished project: Philosophie de la
    volonté
    Vol. I.   Le volontaire et l'involontaire (1950)
    Vol. II. Finitude et culpabilité (1960)
        Part 1. L'homme faillible
        Part 2. La symbolique du mal

B. Subsequent publications:
    De l'interprétation: Essai sur Freud (1965)
        (includes the "Lecture de Freud")

    Le conflit des interprétations (1969)

This table makes clear the importance of the Philosophie de la volonté not only to L'homme faillible, for which it pro- vides the context, but also to De l'interprétation, for which it sets the stage.[20] Accordingly it is upon the Philosophie that our survey of Ricoeur will focus.

It is common knowledge that among the formative in- fluences upon Ricoeur's early work are the existentialist themes and the phenomenological method which were in the ascendant in France during the period when the Philosophie was first conceived. But the concerns of the Philosophie range well beyond its immediate setting. For Ricoeur's confrontation with existentialism became the occasion for an extended debate with the entire dualist tradition which traces back at least as far as Descartes and which finds its great- est recent champion in (the early) Jean-Paul Sartre. This caution regarding the dualist penchant of much existentialist thought is reflected in two of Ricoeur's early themes. The first is his concern that in existentialism human transcend- ence has been so overvalued that, in the end, it becomes definitive of the human. The second theme is the converse of the first, namely a concern that human finitude has been so undervalued that finally it is fused with guilt. Ricoeur writes with regard to "finitude" and "guilt":

> I had the impression, or even the conviction, that
> these two terms tended to be identified in classi-
> cal existentialism at the cost of both experiences,
> guilt becoming a particular case of finitude and
> for that reason beyond cure and forgiveness, and
> finitude, on the other hand, being affected by a
> kind of diffused sense of sadness and despair
> through guilt.[21]

Ricoeur's determination to counter these twin aspects of what we may call a "gnostic" drift in the thought of the time pro- vides a key to the Philosophie de la volonté.

In the initial volume of the Philosophie the first phase of Ricoeur's rebuttal predominates. Le volontaire et l'in- volontaire deflates an overvaluation of human transcendence by showing how, in case after case, the voluntary and the involuntary are interlaced and interdependent. Across a spectrum comprising at the one end free decision and, at the other end, the "experienced necessity" of one's charac- ter, one's unconscious and one's birth, Ricoeur argues that human transcendence, so far from being betrayed, is sup-

ported and sustained by its hold upon the involuntary or finite. In effect, human transcendence requires the "traction"
that human finitude provides. To exalt transcendence at the
expense of the finite is thus to pursue a will-o'-the-wisp; it
is an instance of misplaced concreteness. Worse than that,
it is an instance of misplaced humanity. [22]

While the "et" of Le volontaire et l'involontaire signals interdependence, the "et" of Finitude et culpabilité announces contrast, in keeping with the second phase of Ricoeur's on-going quarrel with the gnostic mode. The difference is dramatized by the second volume's appearing in
separately bound parts, L'homme faillible dealing particularly with finitude and La symbolique du mal dealing particularly with guilt. Yet the lessons of the first volume are not
set aside; here as elsewhere the richness of Ricoeur's work
arises from its being cumulative, not merely consecutive.
Thus L'homme faillible resumes, in a key more expressive
of human tragedy and tornness, the argument mounted in Le
volontaire et l'involontaire. First it shows that even as
viewed under the sign of pathos, which is the birth-sign of
existentialism, our experience continues to display the same
interweaving of the finite and the transcendent--of the finite
and the "infinite." At the same time we also discover that
even these boundary situations of conflict and tragedy do not
of themselves explain the occurrence of evil. Thus in
L'homme faillible the broadly phenomenological method initiated in Le volontaire et l'involontaire finds its most full-
some realization--and an intentional échec. [23]

From this conscious failure of method Ricoeur draws
a substantive conclusion which secures his second line of attack against the gnosticizing strain. The limitations of
L'homme faillible suggest that by examining the structures
of human existence we can attain no more than certain preconditions for the occurrence of moral evil. These preconditions are the "fragility" or "frailty" which is an important
connotation of Ricoeur's "faillibilité." But to be fragile is
not yet to break; the impetus plunging us into moral evil is
not generated by our structures per se. And thus it cannot
be blamed upon them. Finitude is not to be confused with
guilt.

The lesson drawn from the incapacity of one method
in L'homme faillible is reinforced by the fact that when, in
La symbolique du mal, Ricoeur does succeed in engaging the
actuality of moral evil, it is by a different method which

looks to a different place. La symbolique du mal exchanges
phenomenology for a hermeneutical method which looks to
religious symbols, through which the believer has confessed
complicity in evil.   Just as L'homme faillible reaches forward only as far as certain preconditions, still before the
fact, so La symbolique du mal can push back no further than
to an irreducibly symbolic testimony spoken after the damage
has been done.   That the actual occurrence of moral evil is
finally a mystery eluding rational explanation is dramatized
by its falling, as it were, "between" the separately bound
volumes--unencompassed by the reflections of either. [24]

c.   mystery & method

      The mystery of evil in Finitude et culpabilité was an-
ticipated by another mystery in Le volontaire et l'involontaire.   In his Introduction to the earlier work Ricoeur calls
for a method which would demand, finally, that "je participe
activement à mon incarnation comme mystère."   He goes on
to explain:

          La méditation de l'oeuvre de Gabriel Marcel est
          en effet à l'origine des analyses de ce livre;
          toutefois nous avons voulu mettre cette pensée à
          l'épreuve des problèmes précis posés par la
          psychologie classique (problème du besoin, de
          l'habitude etc.); d'autre part nous avons voulu
          nous placer à l'intersection de deux exigences:
          celle d'une pensée alimentée au mystère de mon
          corps, celle d'une pensée soucieuse des distinc-
          tions héritées de la méthode husserlienne de
          description. [25]

No passage better exemplifies the marriage of expansiveness
and rigor which is Ricoeur's own peculiar method.   By sub-
mitting Marcel's elusive questions to Husserl's meticulous
method, Ricoeur means to surmount a split which has been
recurrent in recent philosophy.   Too often existential concerns have led philosophers to a loose, quasi-literary mode
of expression; and conversely, methodological rigor has frequently lent itself to a certain narrowing of subject matter.
Let us look briefly at what Ricoeur has drawn from each of
the key figures: Gabriel Marcel, the Christian existentialist, and Edmund Husserl, the father of phenomenological
method.   The inquiry will extend our discussion of the ricoeurian background and will introduce certain themes

specific to the present study. Our exposition will, of necessity, be highly condensed. [26]

    A "mystery" for Marcel is a question which is reflec-
tive, and endlessly so, because it is a question which impli-
cates the person who is questioning. But it is not solely a
matter of that person's subjectivity, nor is it even primarily
so. This point is entirely crucial if existentialism is not to
be hopelessly subjectivized and thereby removed from the
arena of serious discourse. A facile romanticism has been
oblivious to this distinction. Determined to exalt the existential posture to the level of the ineffable, it has succeeded
in collapsing the existential vocabulary into the trivial. Thus
in common parlance "existential" now means "experiential
with pretensions." As corrective to this sad state, the words
of one commentator are precious. "The metaphysical
mystery of existence," writes H. J. Blackham, "... is not
to be explored beyond the world of having but lies in the
mid-region between having and being, between me and my
life, between the self and the world."[27] Thus mystery is
emphatically not to be equated with a subjective experience
which is hurled in the face of a skeptical objectivity. Mystery rather resides 1) in the logically awkward necessity of
retaining both of two incommensurable viewpoints or languages, viz., my body as lived body and my body as object;
and 2) in the abiding perplexity over how the two relate.
This linguistic embarrassment, which we shall speak of as
an irreducible duality, together with the inexhaustible question of relationship--for mystery is not flatly opaque but
endless--may serve as an abstract guideline for our discussions of the original marcellian concept.

    Having thus corrected the common understanding of
existentialism in a direction more congenial to phenomenology, we may now turn to the other member of Ricoeur's
proposed marriage--to Husserl and the remarkable way in
which his phenomenology, for all its distinctiveness of manner, makes common cause with existentialism. [28] For the
heart of Husserl's endeavor is the brave proposal that subjectivity is the concrete. This concrete was the ground upon
which a variety of traditional dualisms were to be reconciled.
We have just warned of the dangers to which an elevation of
subjectivity falls prey; but for Husserl the identification of
subjectivity with the concrete is not a peremptory collapsing
of terms, it is a goal to be worked toward and a premise
to be vindicated gradually, in the effect. Thus his project
is shielded from abuse by its notorious rigor, but also by

its commitment to comprehensiveness, a comprehensiveness such that subjectivity becomes the correlate of all that presents itself.   Ricoeur, however, is alive to the irony that something essential to human subjectivity may be lost by virtue of that very comprehensiveness !   This something may be what Marcel has spoken of as the sense that one's experience is one's own.   Ricoeur's adoption in Le volontaire et l'involontaire of the will as the index of subjectivity announces his resolve to respect this ingredient of human experience, even if the price be a loss of comprehensiveness and the persistence of a certain duality.   In this duality we find a premonition of mystery in the very act by which Ricoeur condones the prospect which Husserl resisted to the end: the thought that phenomenology's mode of comprehension and its goal of comprehensiveness might finally be at odds.

Thus Ricoeur's fusion of Marcel and Husserl issues in a methodological decision which is reflected by the very title of Le volontaire et l'involontaire.   That work becomes an effort to explore inductively the extent to which the "involuntary"--both the affective and the objective, and thus elements of both Marcel's languages--can be coaxed onto a single plane of discourse which is presided over by an abiding relation, however tenuous, with the "voluntary."[29] We have already noted that the book's immediate aim in this exploration, the aim which is evident when the work is read in isolation from its companion volumes, is to demonstrate against the dualist tradition from Descartes to Sartre the vast continent of experience across which the voluntary and the involuntary relate and cooperate.   But to explore this domain so fully is also to exhibit its limits and such limits may be an index to mystery.   Let us see whether by keeping an eye to this fact and willfully running counter to Ricoeur's immediate aim, by reading him upstream as it were, we may not bring to light a longer-range intent.

Ricoeur introduces a method which he calls the "diagnostique" as a technique appropriate to his immediate aim of meshing the voluntary and the involuntary.[30]   The device amounts to a way of helping phenomenological method along by giving it a hint.   When phenomenology has been pressed to its apparent limits Ricoeur brings to bear the testimony of another party, an objective viewpoint, as a means of supplementing what consciousness reflecting upon its own voluntary activity has found to be directly accessible.   The phenomenologist can then use this outside testimony as a clue to aspects of experience which it has overlooked, but which the method, thus prompted, might yet succeed in laying bare. Thus for example Ricoeur adopts as a diagnostic clue the testimony of the psychoanalyst, and he has some success in achieving by this means an introspective awareness of the unconscious. [31]

Nevertheless, just as Ricoeur's phenomenology had its limits, so does phenomenology assisted by the "diagnostique." The method eventually attenuates to an imaginative appropriation scarcely distinguishable from the imaginative projection which will characterize the La symbolique du mal. Thus, of the biologist's testimony:

> Je dois sans cesse me répéter que mon hérédité n'est que mon caractère mis hors de moi, c'est-à-dire le mode fini de ma liberté aliéné dans l'ancêtre. [32]

Not to speak, as Ricoeur hardly does, of the physicist and the chemist. These limits of the "diagnostique" must be taken to mark the boundaries of the continent of correlation which Ricoeur undertook to explore. His achievement is massively impressive, but in the end the languages of lived body and body-object must go their separate ways.

Can we discern in this conclusion, which Ricoeur does not emphasize, the shadow of a longer-range intent? Let us recall the two guidelines which we enumerated for the marcellian concept of mystery: the irreconcilability of diverse languages and the inexhaustibility of their relationship. Had Ricoeur chosen to come at the mystery of the body primarily by way of the first of these, he might have fostered the impression that he was capitulating to the metaphysical dualists. Therefore he preferred to stress the more affirmative truth, the conceptual expression of the experience of participation, the richness of concrete relationships. But even so, his method at its limits continued tacitly to recognize and to draw upon the correlative guideline, the final division of languages. In a manner which anticipates the échec of Ricoeur's method in L'homme faillible, Le volontaire et l'involontaire is as important for what it does not do as for what it does. The phenomenology which Husserl had fashioned to reconcile all dualisms has worked, in Ricoeur's adaptation, to the retention of a certain duality.

Turning from Le volontaire et l'involontaire to La

symbolique du mal, we may be able to delineate Ricoeur's
method in that work by means of a few comparisons and contrasts. The two books share a tactic which is common to
Ricoeur: the basic framework in each is a spectrum which
runs from the most reflective phenomenon to the least reflective. In _Le volontaire et l'involontaire_ this takes the
form of a spectrum ranging from the freely willed act to
those occasions such as one's birth which are least voluntary
and which most require the testimony of an external obser-
ver. In _La symbolique du mal_ an analogous spectrum ranges
from the "concept," such as original sin or the bound will,
through the "primary symbols"; and these symbols themselves
open up to display a subset ranging from the "pure symbol"
exemplified in "guilt" through the least reflective of all,
namely the "primitive symbol" which looks upon involvement
in evil as a quasi-physical defilement. [33]

Now among these options we, the contemporary readers of _La symbolique du mal_, are apt to gravitate toward the
more reflective pole. "Guilt" will seem a more fitting term
than "defilement," and some concept, drawn perhaps from
psychology or existentialism, may seem the most appropriate
approach of all. In short, we may naturally prefer the demythologized point of view. But this means that the reader
of _La symbolique du mal_ is in a position formally similar to
that of the phenomenologist in _Le volontaire et l'involontaire_.
Both are spontaneously drawn to the "higher" end of the spectrum; both reach toward the "lower" as toward a realm of
opaque and obdurate otherness--the sheer givenness of one's
birth, the crude literalism of the primitive symbol. So we
have a dictum: the extent to which _La symbolique du mal_
marks a real methodological advance over _Le volontaire et
l'involontaire_ may be measured by its success in springing
itself out of this shared predicament.

La symbolique du mal accomplishes such transcendence
of viewpoint in its being able to discern a positive significance
in the offensive symbols, such as the primitive's near-identi-
fication of sin with physical uncleanness. In this book Ricoeur regards such literalism as a tacit witness to the very
thing which the rationalist would too readily overlook, namely
evil's fundamental absurdity. [34] In like fashion _La symbolique
du mal_ can also assign positive significance to the partial irreconcilability of the primary symbol, the pure symbol and
the concept: the diverse languages or viewpoints which make
up the "symbolique." For the whole uneasy field of the
"symbolique," quite including the partial irreconcilability of

its elements, is understood to constitute a cumulative depiction of the phenomenon of evil in both its partial transparency and its final opacity.

Indeed--and this is decisive for our purposes--the entire field of the "symbolique" is the only depiction which is
adequate. For Ricoeur it is no fluke of cultural history that
even the most reflective texts preserve a vestige of the literal. The retention of the literal is significant, for thereby
the demythologized viewpoint confesses itself finally inadequate and gestures beyond itself toward the entirety of the
"symbolique." And the retention is necessary because the
concept of evil in its purity, the rarefied concept of the ser-
vile will with no admixture of the literal, explodes into conceptual contradiction. [35]

Thus the entire "symbolique" is the only adequate depiction. But the depiction is not a single representation;
it may not be taken in a single embrace. The "symbolique,"
after all, is only a composite term for several modes of
discourse which are no less antagonistic for their being interdependent. What has been concluded in principle to be a
depiction remains in practice indissociable from the technique which gives access to it.

This chastening conclusion accords with the understanding of hermeneutics operative throughout La symbolique
du mal. For hermeneutics in this work is the effort to
relate disparate viewpoints or languages without necessarily
resolving them within one descriptive view (thus a difference
from phenomenology) and without subsuming them within a
prescriptive third (whence a difference from at least some
forms of metaphysics). But this is to say that while Le
volontaire et l'involontaire and La symbolique du mal are
alike in their trafficking in spectrums, they differ decisively
in the uses to which the spectrum are put. In Le volontaire
et l'involontaire an antecedent commitment to a unity of
viewpoint set the stage for the "diagnostique," a device which
found alternative viewpoints provisionally useful but finally
dispensable. For all its modifications of phenomenological
technique, this early work continues to side with the fundamental husserlian drive toward a unitary point of view;
"... pour la description et la compréhension, l'un est la
raison du multiple."[36] But La symbolique du mal is another
matter. Here the irreducibility of even the naivest account
and the recognition that this irreducibility has its own positive significance have led Ricoeur to countenance and even
to affirm and celebrate a stubborn pluralism of tongues.

Thus the "diagnostique" and the "symbolique" embody alternative ways of dealing with differences. Against the background of these alternative models, we can now antici- pate the argument which will inform our analyses of L'homme faillible and the "Lecture de Freud." In each of these writ- ings Ricoeur in effect professes the model of the "symbol- ique"--but his method inclines toward the "diagnostique." He avows pluralism, he admonishes us sternly to this effect; and yet his method presses by a logic of its own toward an impe- rialism of the intellect. For this reason I undertake to re- construct each of these writings to offset that tendency and to achieve a more even-handed account. In various contexts the stakes in such reconstruction are variously formulable as "pluralism," "duality" or "mystery."[37]

For the present, however, it is enough to summarize our discussion of "mystery & method" by noting that where- as the phenomenology of Le volontaire et l'involontaire neces- sarily proved inadequate to one mystery, namely that of the body, the hermeneutics of La symbolique du mal has proved adequate to another, that of evil--but at the price that method and matter have fused inseparably so that the mystery is never comprehended independently and synoptically, but only in the on-going business of interpretation.

d. tactics

The philosopher Gilles Deleuze has remarked, "On n'écrit qu'à la pointe de son savoir, à cette pointe extrême qui sépare notre savoir et notre ignorance, et qui fait pas- ser l'un dans l'autre."[38] This study in the thought of Paul Ricoeur seeks to examine an important writer "à la pointe de son savoir." We presume to speak of "the" central is- sues in a thinker whose work is as overdetermined as the symbols to which he attends. And we presume to show that the logic so located directs us beyond and even against cer- tain of Ricoeur's explicit pronouncements. This bringing to light of certain implications which Ricoeur himself only ad- umbrates will require, if it is to be at all persuasive, a long process of close textual argument. The effort may per- haps serve as a tribute to the richness of Ricoeur's accom- plishment. Certainly analysis of this sort would seem a necessary step if his style of thinking is to be appropriated in the very different philosophic climate which prevails on this side of the English Channel.

A number of steps have been taken to make this format accessible to the general reader. The General Conclusion and subsidiary Conclusions are clearly marked. Cross-references indicate some essential connections within the book and there is an index to supplement these cross-references. Page references to Ricoeur are generally given within the text rather than in footnotes.[39] Underlining is used rather liberally, and French and English have been mixed shamelessly; my sole criterion in such matters has been ease of comprehension.

One form of encouragement, however, the reader has been denied. I have found it impossible to strew the text with the customary clues and enticements; I have not been able to furnish the reassuring proleptic leaps which emerge from matters at hand to survey the ultimate purposes. This breach of etiquette is, I think, a function of our argument. It would be relatively easy to propose a priori that a certain concept of mystery be applied to Ricoeur, and then to back up the decision by showing that the concept "throws light upon" his various works. But that approach tends to smudge the distinctions between what is our contrivance, what is properly Ricoeur's and what may arise from the object of study itself. Even for a study "of" Ricoeur the tactic would be uncertain; for our own effort, which would subordinate the study of Ricoeur to other substantive concerns, a more inductive approach seems preferable. One can never completely shake free of one's presuppositions, of course; but at least we may keep to a minimum the intrusion of our own agenda by saying that as a rule only those questions will be put to Ricoeur's text which might occur to any inquisitive reader. Thus discussion of mystery and of theological implications will be reserved for the various Conclusions.

The reader does have at hand, however, a conceptual compass which will place the most derivative issue in its relation to our initial purpose. We began by resolving that no aspect of human experience should be dismissed as unworthy or incapable of theological attention. With Auden we would "unite / the unequal moieties fractured / by our own well-meaning sense of justice...." Thus to determine what is at stake in any of our discussions one need only look to the fate of these allegedly "lower" aspects of experience. They are: among the levels treated in L'homme faillible, the emotions; among the emotions, pleasure; in the freudian topographies, the pleasure principle; and in the late theory of the instincts, those agencies most resistant to social accord.

These, in Auden's words, are the "long-forgotten objects"
which "lie in the grass of our neglect." Our championing of
these elements is similar to certain concerns of recent feminist theologians. [40] In the context of our own study, it sets
the stage for a concept of mystery which would enjoy valid-
ity not despite the operations of these elements, but because
of them. And yet the question of the status of these aspects
of our experience is a matter which might suggest itself to
any reader of Ricoeur. For Ricoeur--and behind Ricoeur,
Freud--both vow an intent to do justice to these sides of experience. It is natural to ask whether they succeed; and if
they do not, to ask how they might.

It has been said of Freud that he discovered what every wet-nurse already knew; and it is true of our own study
that throughout the abstract discussions, one eye will be fixed
upon certain rather homely concerns. But is is among these,
too, that the human lot is cast. And who knows but that even
they may take us rather far, if only they be earnestly ques-
tioned and roundly affirmed?

* * *

It is a pleasant task to acknowledge my indebtedness
to Professor Edward Farley for introducing me to phenomenology, to Professor James M. Gustafson for encouraging my
interest in Ricoeur, and to Professor Julian N. Hartt for
years of counsel and support. I wish to add a special note
of gratitude to Professor Don Ihde, who made available to me
his study on Ricoeur while it was still in manuscript form.

The preparation of this work has been supported at
various stages by a Fulbright-Hayes Fellowship, a Danforth
Fellowship and a grant from The Association of Theological
Schools in the United States and Canada. Without this gen-
erous assistance, the way would have been longer and more
difficult.

The poetry which appears at various points in the text
is in all cases drawn from W. H. Auden's "In Memory of
Sigmund Freud."[41] My thanks to Random House for permission to quote. And to Éditions Aubier Montaigne and
Éditions du Seuil, my thanks for their kind permission to
quote from L'homme faillible and De l'interprétation, respectively.

PART   1

THE STRUCTURE OF CONSCIOUSNESS
IN L'HOMME FAILLIBLE

while, as they lie in the grass of our neglect,
    so many long-forgotten objects
    revealed by his undiscouraged shining

are returned to us and made precious again;
games we had thought we must drop as we grew up,
    little noises we dared not laugh at,
    faces we made when no one was looking.

INTRODUCTION

L'homme faillible continues to hold a central place among Ricoeur's writings. It sets forth Ricoeur's vision of the human condition in a manner which is remarkably encompassing and yet relatively accessible. To penetrate to the heart of this brief book is to have gone far toward understanding Ricoeur. As regards our own purposes, the work may provide a model of conscious experience to compare and contrast with our eventual study of the unconscious; and more specifically it may offer a first instance of "mystery" to clarify that concept before we enter the more elusive world of psychoanalysis. Let us begin, then, by examining the author's purpose and his means of carrying it forward.

a. "faillibilité": Ricoeur's purpose

Asking about Ricoeur's purpose is a way of scouting out the terrain. Such caution is well advised, for the landscape is rich but also bewildering in the luxuriance of its terminological foliage. This conceptual density may account for a certain baroque quality which occasionally creeps into Ricoeur commentaries, and even into the writings of Ricoeur himself. Faced with this embarrassment of riches, we may take the author's announced purpose as an initial guide in sorting the central from the peripheral concerns. Certainly a writer's intent cannot be the final word upon the logical structure of a work. But it is an important indication; and if such assistance has been offered, we shall have reason to be grateful.

One suggestion about the purpose of L'homme faillible has already been made on the basis of its function within the larger context of the Philosophie de la volonté. In that light the work appears as a rebuttal of the tendency on the part of much existentialist thought to so exalt human transcendence that human finitude, so contrasted, becomes confused with guilt. On Ricoeur's view a successful response to this

tendency must tread the line of affirming human participation
in evil while yet avoiding the fatal identification of finitude
with guilt.   It is to this requirement that the concept of
"finitude" responds.   Thus if one follows Ricoeur's translator
in rendering "faillibilité" by its English cognate "fallibility, "
one should also bear in mind the translator's insistence that
this be glossed by another term, namely "fault. "   And "fault"
in this work is understood in a manner akin to the geological
usage, as "a break, a rift, a tearing. "[1]   "Faillibilité" thus
suggests not a recurrent act, an occasional lapse into wrong-
doing, but a structural characteristic of the human makeup
which stops short of engendering, by itself, any specific act.
In this light a translation of "faillibilité" as "frailty" or
"fragility" may be useful in indicating that what is intended
is a necessary but not sufficient condition for the realization
of moral evil.

        These reflections, however, are drawn from a per-
spective which remains somewhat extrinsic to the volume at
hand.   It remains to determine how L'homme faillible would
understand itself.   Here the section entitled "L'hypothèse de
travail" is especially pertinent.   For the "Avant-propos"
which opens the work is given over to a discussion of the
relationship of L'homme faillible to other volumes of the
Philosophie de la volonté, particularly La symbolique du mal;
and the section which follows the "hypothèse" is already a
stage within the study itself.

        While the "hypothèse" may thus afford the best point
of entry for a discussion of L'homme faillible, it should be
read in the awareness that it is something of a polemical
tract.   The concept of "faillibilité" is prominent from the
first lines of the "hypothèse"; and Ricoeur writes,

        Ma seconde hypothèse de travail ... est que ce
        caractère global consiste dans une certaine non-
        coïncidence de l'homme avec lui-même; cette
        'disproportion' de soi à soi serait la ratio de la
        faillibilité.   (21)[2]

The polemical target of this formulation is soon evident.   It
is a long-standing tradition which views the human as half-
angel and half-beast, the offspring of contrary realms, at
home in neither and forever hovering restlessly between the
two.   To be human is to be a paradoxical crossing of the
finite and the infinite, an intermediary between two worlds
(22).   In criticism of this view, Ricoeur contends,

... dire que l'homme est situé entre l'être et le
néant, c'est déjà traiter la réalité humaine comme
une région, comme un lieu ontologique, comme
une place logée entre d'autres places; or ce schème
de l'intercalation est fort trompeur: il invite à
traiter l'homme comme un objet dont la place
serait repérée par rapport à d'autres réalités plus
ou moins complexes que lui ... (22-23, emphases
Ricoeur's)

Thus Ricoeur insists, "c'est en lui-même, de soi à soi qu'il
est intermédiaire" (23).

Now the temptation is to construe Ricoeur's own purpose solely by indirection from this polemical thrust. It
might seem that he is pitting anthropology against metaphysics. One might suppose that he is pressing against the
metaphysical tradition the blanket charge that it is an extrinsic approach which may perhaps begin by simply relating the
human to certain realms, but which ends by assimilating the
human to the status of such realms. Ricoeur would then
seem to have quite turned his back upon the tradition as being hopelessly implicated in the reduction of the human to an
object. On this reading Ricoeur's own proposal would be for
an intrinsic approach ("c'est en lui-même, de soi à soi ...")
and for an approach which would view the human not as object but as activity: "... pour l'homme, être-intermédiaire
c'est faire médiation." (23)

On reexamination, however, the opening lines of Ricoeur's critique may be seen to post a warning against so
simple a reading of his position:

Que nous ne soyons pas en état d'aborder directe-
ment cette caractéristique ontologique de l'homme,
cela n'est pas douteux ... (22, emphasis added)

I would suggest that Ricoeur's quarrel is not with ontology
or metaphysics as such, but only with a framework which is
implemented so hastily or so unreflectively that violence is
done to the special character of the beings in question. In
the present instance that means violence to the special character of our relationship to the various realms of experience.
If there can be an account which avoids this flaw, then ontology may be legitimate. The longer path to ontology, the
indirect route, is the search for such an account. [3]

If we now read Ricoeur's earlier, polemical formula-

tion in the context of this cautionary note, we may arrive at
a fairly balanced account of what it is he is after.   On the
one hand, an approach to human nature should in some sense
be intrinsic, it should delineate a "disproportion" and it
should center upon an activity.   At the same time, for all
its being intrinsic, it should also be relational: it should
faithfully depict the nature of our relationship to the various
realms of experience.   When these considerations are taken
together, one may begin to appreciate the importance for Ricoeur of the concept of "intentionality. "

b.   intentionality: Ricoeur's strategy

        The effect of our discussion of Ricoeur's purpose is
to suggest that of the various concepts and tactics which are
touched upon in "L'hypothèse de travail" and which are implemented in the work at large, a special importance must
attach to "intentionality. "[4]   For here is a perspective on the
human which proposes to be intrinsic, which traces a crucial
disproportion, as we shall see, and which is an activity.   At
the same time the concept is relational: Ricoeur will insist
that even in the case of the emotions, to intend is to intend
some specific correlate.

        It might seem superfluous to so stress the importance
of this phenomenological concept in the thought of one who is
commonly recognized as a phenomenologist.   But in point of
fact Ricoeur wears his phenomenological mantle rather lightly in Finitude et culpabilité and there are passages within
L'homme faillible which might as readily be the work of a
disciple of Kant or a student of hermeneutics.   Indeed two of
the major studies on Ricoeur are concerned to argue that his
is a mixed method incorporating hermeneutical elements along-
side traditional phenomenology. [5]

        So there is good reason to remind oneself of the cen-
trality of "intentionality" in L'homme faillible, and to view
the concept in terms of Ricoeur's purpose as we have sketched
it.   In this light we can now make some observations about
the lay of the land.   First, with regard to the relationship
between L'homme faillible and Le volontaire et l'involontaire,
one may discern a certain continuity and a certain contrast.
The earlier work was a fairly traditional phenomenological
study; thus the two works have in common the theme of intentionality.   But there is an important difference between
the roles which that concept plays.   By and large Le volon-

taire et l'involontaire was content simply to use the concept;
its eye was upon the series of cases which came under study,
rather than upon intentionality itself.   In contrast, the cases
in L'homme faillible are of a very general sort and serve
only as a broad context within which attention is drawn to the
concept of intentionality in its own right--its basic types and
the grounds for its possibility.

In addition, viewing L'homme faillible through the
prism of intentionality gives some orientation with regard to
the crucial question of the relationship between, and the relative status of, the three stages or spheres of study which
constitute that work.   The spheres, anticipated in the last
pages of "L'hypothèse de travail" and reflected in the central
chapters of the book, are "la synthèse transcendentale, " "la
synthèse pratique" and "la fragilité affective"--in effect: the
intellect, the will and the emotions. 6 Of the three, the study
of the intellect ("La synthèse transcendentale") appears first
in the series; and throughout the subsequent explorations of
the will and the emotions, the results of that first study frequently reappear as providing a prototype of some sort (e.g.
107 ff.) In like fashion, Ricoeur's separately published summary of L'homme faillible begins with the intellect; and one
important passage seems to suggest that the spheres of will
and emotion are to be regarded merely as subsidiary examples. 7   But the effect of our own considerations is to indicate that this priority of the intellect is at least partly
methodological.   The intellect is treated first because it
provides the clearest and most accessible illustration of a
larger concern, which is intentionality (cf. 25).   But that
concern, once introduced, may lead one far beyond the realm
of the intellect as such.

To summarize, our reconstruction of Ricoeur's purpose pointed to the centrality of the concept of "intentionality. "   That concept in turn helped clarify the relation of
L'homme faillible to its predecessor; and it threw light on
the relationship between intellect, will and emotion in
L'homme faillible itself.   This last issue trenches upon a
matter crucial to our own initial purpose: the role of hierarchy in the interpretation of human nature, and the recurrent difficulty of giving the supposedly "lower" aspects their
due.   The question of the relative status of intellect, will
and emotion will thus be with us throughout our study of
L'homme faillible, as we probe the manner in which Ricoeur's
strategy is deployed.

THE QUESTION OF FRAMEWORK

Let us ask now, more broadly, what conceptual framework is most basic to L'homme faillible and thus to its portrayal of human nature? The answer would seem to be the polarity of "finite" and "infinite." Ricoeur himself testifies:

> C'est finalement dans cette structure de médiation entre le pôle de finitude et le pôle d'infinitude de l'homme qu'est cherchée la faiblesse spécifique de l'homme et son essentielle faillibilité. (12)

And even more emphatically: "c'est ce rapport qui fait de la limitation humaine le synonyme de la faillibilité." (150, emphasis Ricoeur's) Moreover the "Table des matières" is the mirror of his intent. The chapters on intellect and will are subtitled to reflect this polarity and its mediating term; and the chapters themselves are organized accordingly. [8] Little wonder then that Ricoeur's commentators have been virtually of one voice in adopting the author's own account. It is natural to experience a certain relief upon discovering that a work so various in detail can be surveyed so tidily.

The near-total accord of the author and his commentators requires that I turn a portion of my energies to reopening the case. I shall have to argue that there still is a question about the framework of L'homme faillible. This I propose to do inductively, first by laying out the conventional reading of L'homme faillible and endeavoring in the process to do justice to the very real insights of that point of view. Then I shall raise certain questions about that approach, largely on internal grounds; and I shall spell out an alternative reading based on a different framework. Finally, with the two frameworks fully before us, we may close with an exposition of the way the frameworks interact in the text, and thus in Ricoeur's understanding of human consciousness.

30

I. THE CONCEPTS:
The elements of L'homme faillible

My argument in briefest terms is that intentionality is indeed the key to L'homme faillible, but that the role of intentionality cannot be reduced to the operations of the finite/infinite polarity. It is rather a key which operates in two quite different ways. On the one hand it makes possible the distinction between two types of intention, namely the empty and the fulfilled. On the other hand it calls forth a quite different set of terms which relate not to types of intention but to the foundations of intentionality as such.

The two sets of terms represent two phases of reflection, both of which might enlist under Ricoeur's banner of "transcendental" thought, "c'est-à-dire d'une réflexion qui parte non de moi, mais de l'objet devant moi, et de là, remonte à ses conditions de possibilité. " (25) The first arises as one reasons from certain aspects of the phenomenologically given object to the corresponding acts or aspects of the intending subject. The second bears the mark of a reasoning from the entire intending relationship, subject and object alike, to the conditions necessary for its possibility. I hope to show that these two sets of concepts generate disparate frameworks which are quite equally crucial to a proper comprehension of what Ricoeur is driving at.

a. concepts relating to types of intention

This set of concepts lies at the root of what I have called the "conventional reading" of L'homme faillible. From this source issues the power of that approach to human experience--and also the limitations.

i. "finite" & "infinite"

The substantive issue which defines the conventional reading is its reliance upon the finite/infinite polarity (along with a third, mediating term) as the key to L'homme faillible. Both Don Ihde's Hermeneutic Phenomenology: The Philosophy of Paul Ricoeur and David M. Rasmussen's Mythic-Symbolic Language and Philosophical Anthropology: A Constructive Interpretation of the Thought of Paul Ricoeur subscribe to this approach.   Allowance must be made for the fact that each of these writers is attempting to survey the entirety of Ricoeur's work. And certainly, to speak of a "conventional reading" is not to suggest that the commentators simply retail the categories of "finite" and "infinite" without reflection. Both have fashioned works of original interpretation. But it is to say that what these authors interpret is, by and large, this one abiding polarity as it appears in the realms of intellect, will and emotion.

Thus Rasmussen is suggestive in linking L'homme faillible to Ricoeur's earlier work by a concept of human freedom; but the concept displays itself within L'homme faillible in the portrayal of the human "as constituted between the extremes of transcendence and limitation, finite and infinite."[9] Ihde, for his part, chooses to read Ricoeur against the background of Kant and Husserl. The outcome is highly illuminating; indeed, for just this reason, we are about to adopt Ihde as something of a guide. Only, one reservation may be posted before we do so. Ihde's interpretation is a kantian and husserlian examination of the same finite/infinite polarity; he is a guide within the limits of the conventional view.

Ihde gives to his chapter on L'homme faillible the title "Phenomenology within 'Kantian' Limits." His suggestion is that in L'homme faillible Ricoeur employs Kant to a very specific end: namely, to separate--to make a polarity of--that which in Husserl had been as one. But in tracing this shift there lies a trap for the interpreter. For while Husserl does not separate the topics which we will be considering, he does make a distinction between them. Thus there is already in Husserl all the terminology one would need in order to effect the kantian separation, though the conceptuality is lacking. The result is that the kantian move in Ricoeur, the "limiting" separation, is not always heralded by the influx of a strikingly kantian vocabulary. The persistence of the husserlian terminology obscures the fact that the language is being turned to a different, non-husserlian end. In the interest of clarity, therefore, we may do well to begin with a passage in which Ricoeur posits the separation in terms which are distinctively kantian. Then we can consciously translate from the kantian framework to the husserlian; and on the basis of the interpreted husserlian terminology we can make what further adjustments may be appropriate to the text of L'homme faillible.

Ihde has underscored the importance of the passage in the essay on Kant and Husserl in which Ricoeur insists upon:

... la distinction, fondamentale chez Kant, mais
totalement inconnue chez Husserl, entre l'intention
et l'intuition: Kant dissocie radicalement le rapport
à quelque chose ... et la vision de quelque chose.
Le Etwas = X est une intention sans intuition. 10

What is misleading, as we have said, is that, contra Ricoeur,
Husserl was not ignorant of the distinction as such; it is the possibility of a dissociation or separation which is alien to him and
peculiar to Kant. Ihde makes this point incidentally in a passage
which bears us a step nearer to our goal:

Translating this limitation back into husserlian terms
is to say that an intention need not be fulfilled (empty
intentions, for example). Ricoeur's claim, however,
is stronger and in effect means that all intentions
stop short of total fulfillment. 11

Yet in none of this is Ricoeur simply following Kant for
Kant's sake. One need only recall our discussion of Ricoeur's
purpose in L'homme faillible. Much of the importance of the
concept of intentionality for Ricoeur lies in its capacity for portraying the human as an activity. The importance of Kant, in
turn, is in securing an understanding of intentionality as such
an activity. This task might appear superfluous in light of Husserl's frequent reference to "intentional acts," but here again
appearances are deceptive. For to the extent that there is in
Husserl no separation--no pause, as it were--between the intention and the intuition, the act becomes instantaneous and the
sense of calling it an "act" at all becomes uncertain. The effect of Ricoeur's kantian separation is permanently to insure
against the collapsing of intention and intuition into one, and
thereby to guard against a threatened evacuation of the concept
of intentional activity.

Our promised translation from Kant to Husserl is not yet
complete. For what Ricoeur has called, in a kantian context, a
separation of "intention" from "intuition" may be characterized
in husserlian terms as a separation between two senses of "intention." This occurs when "intention" is taken in a broad
sense, similar to the manner in which we have spoken of "intentionality." Thus Ricoeur observes in another essay that for
Husserl,

... la conscience est ainsi doublement intentionnelle,
une première fois à titre de signification, une deu-
xième fois à titre de remplissement intuitif ... 12

With its next sentence this passage leads into our next step,
translation from Husserl into Ricoeur's own terminology.
The sentence is in apposition to the husserlian lines just
quoted, yet its vocabulary is almost identical to that of
L'homme faillible: Ricoeur says of Husserl, "dans les pre-
mières oeuvres, la conscience est à la fois parole et perception". [13] Just so, in L'homme faillible Ricoeur roots his discussion of the intellect in the dialectic between one's signify-
ing speech and one's perspectival perception (35-63, passim).

    Our translation has thus traced the linkage between
Kant and Ricoeur by way of Husserl. Let us see how the
kantian connection pays off in a reading of Ricoeur. To do
so, one need only set the finite/infinite polarity, upon which
Ricoeur has so insisted, in tandem with the present polarity
of intuition and intention, respectively. On the conventional
reading virtually all of L'homme faillible is born of this
alignment. It is by allowing these polarities to interpret one
another that Ricoeur arrives at his characteristic middle
course. For on the one hand it was the burden of "L'hypothèse de travail" that left to themselves, without some form of
mediation, the categories of "finite" and "infinite" exhibit a
centrifugal, dualistic drive. And, on the other hand, it is
the common lament of the existentialist critic that the early
Husserl set a monistic imprint upon the concept of intentionality. Might it not be that if the two polarities were properly wedded, their respective penchants toward dualism and
monism would cancel each other out?

    This proposal lends L'homme faillible much of its co-
herence and its dynamic. Behind the proposal lies the thought
that once the finite has been seen as intuitive fulfillment, it
will become clear that what is honorifically called the "infinite" is still in some sense partial. The infinite needs the
finite as intention needs intuitive fulfillment; there is no warrant for exhalting the infinite to a proud and finally dualistic
isolation. Thus the book's coherence. (The formulation is
of obvious pertinence to our considerations regarding the role
of hierarchy in an understanding of human nature.) Conversely, there is behind Ricoeur's proposal the further thought that
once it has been understood that intuitive fulfillment is con-
stitutionally finite, incomplete, and that in contrast intention
is in principle infinite, it will become clear that an intuition
can never become coextensive with its intention. Whence the
book's dynamic: the consequence of Ricoeur's claim that, in
Ihde's words, "all intentions stop short of total fulfillment"[14]
is that intention and intuition can never collapse into one, as

is their tendency in the early Husserl's treatment of intentional activity.

In carrying out this proposal the case of the <u>intellect</u> is, as we have noted, the point of departure and in <u>some</u> undetermined sense the abiding paradigm. The reasons for Ricoeur's choice of starting point are significant for the study at large. They appear to be, first, that the intellect is a clearer, more manageable topic than the will or the emotions (35); and secondly that with regard to any faculty it is less confusing to begin with the corresponding object, as it presents itself, rather than plunge directly into the abyss of introspection (36). Together the premises point us to the <u>object</u> which presents itself to the <u>intellect</u>. Ricoeur speaks in this connection of "la réflexion 'transcendantale'" (35). Teutonic overtones notwithstanding, Ricoeur's starting point would seem in the present perspective to be a characteristically Gallic passion for clarity; and the fact that he then proceeds to extend his paradigm to the will and the emotions would seem to illustrate an equally Gallic predilection for quasi-deductive argument.

Given this starting point then, how does Ricoeur proceed? The answer would seem to lie, as we have suggested, in the marriage of two polarities, the finite/infinite and the intuition/intention. For it is this conjunction which enables Ricoeur to raise the intellect's object as a <u>problem</u>, as a question for study, without having it topple over into a state of hopeless paradox. The first half of this task, the posing of the problem, is the work of the first members of the two polarities. For beginning the study of "La synthèse transcendantale" with "la perspective finie" as Ricoeur does may be understood as a device for raising the problem, a means of extricating the object from the plane of the all-too-obvious. [15] It would be tempting to suggest that Ricoeur does this by beginning with the object as it appears to us ("la perspective finie") and then proceeding toward the object as it is in itself. But the suggestion is freighted with presuppositions which are foreign to Ricoeur. A philosophic study may begin with an awareness of finite perspective, but one's spontaneous consciousness does not. It is only secondarily, after the rude shock of finding oneself in error, that consciousness acquires an awareness, indeed a wariness, of the perspectival character of perception (39).

But with that wariness the intellect's object does become a problem indeed--it seems to melt into incoherence.

Perception comes to seem nothing more than a staccato of
disjointed perspectives.   Accordingly it is at this point that
Ricoeur calls upon the countervailing members of his polarities.   Or rather it is at this point that Ricoeur remarks
that in the course of the discussion of perspective the poles
of intention and infinity have been constantly presupposed.

> C'est sur la chose même que je transgresse égale-
> ment ma perspective.   En effet je ne puis dire
> cette unilatéralité qu'en disant toutes les faces que
> je ne vois pas actuellement ...   (44, emphases Ri-
> coeur's)

On this passage, two remarks.   First, it indicates that by
"infinite" Ricoeur means something rather modest.   His usage
of "infinite" follows directly from the assumption that it is of
the essence of finitude to be bound to some partial, perspectival view.   The character of infinity thus lies in that aspect
of the intellect which is independent of any particular perspective; the "infinite" is simply the aperspectival. [16]   Secondly,
the passage clearly locates this transcendence of perspective
in our ability to speak, and specifically in our ability to make
judgments.

Considered in the abstract, "la perspective finie" and
"le verbe infini" stand in considerable tension; as Ricoeur
puts it, there is a "disproportion" (55).   And yet the concrete object presents itself as a synthesis, a "synthèse du
sens et de l'apparence" (56).   This fact persuades Ricoeur
of the necessity of a third, intermediary term, which he calls,
in kantian fashion, "l'imagination pure" (55 f.).   And when
all is said and done, the fact which initially justified the
third term is virtually its definition as well.   For:

> ... ce troisième terme n'est pas susceptible de
> se réflechir comme la sensibilité s'est réflechie
> dans la conscience de perspective et comme le
> verbe s'est réflechi dans la conscience de signi-
> fication, puis dans la conscience d'affirmation.
> L'étonnant est que ce troisième terme n'est pas
> donné en lui-même, mais seulement dans la chose
> (55).

And what is "donné ... seulement dans la chose" is the
thing's objectivity, the fact of there being a synthesis: in
sum, the fact which led Ricoeur to postulate a mediating
term in the first place.

We have dwelt at some length upon a single chapter of L'homme faillible, "La synthèse transcendantale," because the joining of the polarity of "finite" and "infinite" with the distinction between intuition and intention constitutes the heart of the conventional view, and because the case of "perspective" and "word" is the paradigm of that conjunction. It tells much about the conventional view that, in order to complete its reading of L'homme faillible, one need only extend that same pattern to the realms of the will and the emotions. The extensions are required because, after all, the intellect is only one abstracted aspect of consciousness;[17] and it is legitimate because:

> Ce que le sentiment manifeste, par le moyen des accents affectifs visés sur les choses, c'est l'intentionnalité même des tendances ... (102)

"Cette thèse," Ricoeur adds, "est la pierre angulaire de toute notre réflexion ..." (102). Once again the conventional view seems to be firmly warranted by the writer's own remarks.

Of course it takes a certain amount of ingenuity to make the extensions work and a large part of any conventional exposition must be expended in the task; but therein lies the very fascination of L'homme faillible. And so, sooner or later, "character" and "humanity," and then "pleasure" and "happiness," are jockeyed into the positions which were originally filled by the polarity of "perspective" and "word." We will have a closer look at how this is accomplished in a particular case when we undertake our "explication de texte."[18] For the present it is enough to note with regard to these extensions not that they are in any sense wrong-- for indeed they are true to Ricoeur, they depict some of his best insights, and even when retailed at second hand they are capable of striking the reader as something of a tour de force--but that they are indeed a matter of filling conceptual slots. From beginning to end they are carried off without the introduction of a single new category or mode of thought.

ii.   the framework: its possible limitations

To wish to look beyond the conventional view, it is not necessary to have placed that view definitively.[19] One need only suspect that the view suffers certain limitations. One need only be disturbed by certain questions.

Thus far we have seen that the conventional reading
of L'homme faillible posits nothing more than a purely logical relationship between the several spheres of human nature
or of human experience, the spheres of intellect, of will and
of emotion: each sphere or level has a structure and between the structures there are certain analogies. Our first
question then is to ask whether, beyond the purely formal
relationships, there might not exist some further structure
which relates the spheres or levels and somehow accounts
for their interaction. Offhand one would think that there
must be; and Ricoeur affirms that there is. As we shall
see in greater detail in our next section, Ricoeur repeatedly
drops two explicit clues about that embracing relationship:
it is a relationship between abstraction and concreteness, and
it is a relationship between consciousness and self-consciousness. (In almost every case the context of these remarks is
an explanation of what it is that is uniquely contributed to
human experience by the emotions, and so it is upon the
emotions that the next section will concentrate.)[20]

But first we need to consider a second question which
follows from our answer to the first. Does the conventional
view have the resources to follow out these clues? Certainly references to the concrete and the like can be found in
conventional expositions of Ricoeur: in effect, the expositions
repeat the clues.[21] But merely to repeat the clues is already to suggest that one is able to do no more than repeat,
and the crucial question remains. Specifically we may ask:
given the elements or concepts into which we have analyzed
it (the distinction of "finite" and "infinite" and the correlative types of intention), can the conventional framework give
us an understanding of such notions as "the concrete" and
"self-consciousness," which notions, as we have said, are
in themselves no more than clues? If this crucial question
arouses a certain uneasiness, we have sufficient reason to
look beyond the conventional view.

We can rephrase the question in terms which relate
more expressly to Ricoeur's own text. To do so we need
not abandon Ihde's kantian approach, we need simply take the
approach in earnest; which is to say, we need simply assume
that Ricoeur takes Kant in earnest. The summary comment
which concludes Ricoeur's article comparing Kant and Husserl is that "Husserl fait la phénoménologie. Mais Kant la
limite et la fonde."[22] By way of summary and anticipation,
we ourselves may say of Ricoeur that in Le volontaire et
l'involontaire he did phenomenology; that in L'homme faillible,

according to the best of the conventional readings, he limited
phenomenology--and that there remains the task of grounding
it.

      To this line of attack the conventional view does have
a response. In "L'hypothèse de travail" Ricoeur took as his
method "une réflexion de style 'transcendantal'," which he
characterized as:

> ... une réflexion qui parte non de moi, mais de
> l'objet devant moi, et de là, remonte à ses con-
> ditions de possibilité. (25, cf. 150ff.)

Reflection of this type was in fact given central importance
by the conventional view, as a device for "reading off of the
object" the most fundamental characteristics of the subject;
and certainly, so the response concludes, a way of thinking
which would ground the phenomenological object may succeed
in grounding phenomenology itself.

      The elements of a rejoinder to this defense of the con-
ventional view have already been touched upon. We have already suggested that there may be as much Husserl as Kant
in Ricoeur's definition of transcendental reflection. [23] Of
course Husserl himself derives the tactic from Kant; but if
we are to take seriously Ricoeur's own capsule distinction--
"Husserl fait la phenomenologie. Mais Kant la limite et la
fonde."--we will have to assume that what Husserl shares
with Kant is precisely not that in Kant which is pertinent to
the grounding (or for that matter, the limiting) of phenomenology. We will not get at the grounding of phenomenology by
relying on a term such as "transcendental reflection" which
blurs the distinctions between Husserl and Kant and which
thereby obscures Ricoeur's own reasons for turning from the
one to the other.

      Moreover there is certainly more Husserl than Kant
in the conventional view's interpretation of Ricoeur's original
definition of transcendental reflection. Here we may recall
our observation that there are two quite distinct activities
which march under the banner of "transcendental" thought. [24]
It is one thing to speak of grounding the presentation of the
object by reference to the subject. That is a task which
remains within the bounds of traditional phenomenology and
is indeed achieved, as the conventional view has claimed,
within the conventional reading of L'homme faillible. But it
is something else again to speak, as Ricoeur does in his

reference to Kant, of grounding phenomenology itself.   That
would entail, in the language of L'homme faillible, grounding
the entire subject-object relationship--a task of which the
phenomenological tradition became increasingly conscious,
but which the conventional reading, apart from repeating the
general clues regarding concreteness and self-consciousness,
seems largely to ignore.   It is in this sense that the question
of grounding may prove to be the distinctive task of an alternative approach.

b.   concepts relating to the foundations of intentionality

        In the introduction to his chapter on the emotions Ri-
coeur writes:

    ... l'enjeu d'une philosophie du sentiment, c'est
    l'écart même entre l'exégèse purement transcen-
    dantale de la 'disproportion' et l'épreuve vécue
    de la 'misère' (99).

This is to say that the outcome of the study of the emotions
is important to the question which we have been pressing,
the question of the grounding of the subject-object relationship.   Accordingly the present section will center upon Ricoeur's fourth chapter, "La fragilité affective."

        In speaking of an experience of "la 'misère'" as pro-
viding the criterion against which the description of the intellect may be measured, Ricoeur is referring to an earlier
section of L'homme faillible, namely "le pathétique de la
'misère'" (26-34), a sort of prephilosophical prologue to the
central chapters of the book.   What is crucial, in Ricoeur's
view, is that the quasi-poetic materials of "le pathétique"
are able to evoke the human condition in its entirety and may
therefore be taken as a touchstone of completeness against
which to test the more analytic, philosophic descriptions of
humanity. [25]   The decision to proceed in this manner is consonant with an earlier resolution, which may be quoted in
full.

    Or si le progrès de la pensée, dans une anthro-
    pologie philosophique, ne consiste jamais à aller
    du simple au complexe, mais procède toujours à
    l'intérieur de la totalité même, ce ne peut être
    qu'un progrès dans l'élucidation philosophique de
    la vue globale.   Il faut donc que cette totalité

> soit d'abord donnée en quelque façon avant la philo-
> sophie, dans une précompréhension qui se prête à
> la réflexion ... (24, emphasis Ricoeur's).

That there should be a touchstone and that one should begin
with it is essential to Ricoeur's determination to rule out at
the very beginning any reductionism which would pretend to
reconstruct the human out of lesser elements.

Ricoeur's reference to a hiatus "entre l'exégèse pure-
ment transcendantale de la 'disproportion' et l'épreuve vécue
de la 'misère'" represents a use of the touchstone to criti-
cize both the discussion of the intellect in his second chapter
and the "transcendental" method which presided over that
work. The method is identical with the first of the two pro-
grams which we have distinguished within Ricoeur's transcendental reflection, namely the interpreting of the intending subject in terms of the intended object. Now it is hardly surprising that Ricoeur should find a description of the intellect
to be insufficient as an account of the entirety of human nature; but it is remarkably difficult to say offhand just what
the nature of that insufficiency is, or conversely just what
it is that the emotions bring as their unique contribution to
the human make-up. [26] If a definition of that insufficiency or
incompleteness could be accomplished, however, it might
lead us to an understanding of the limitations of the method
from which the description issued. Then we might know
what would be needed in order to ground that method, and to
ground the subject-object relationship upon which it relies.
Such in any event is the premise upon which our present section will proceed.

Ricoeur gives an initial clue to the nature of the incompleteness when he characterizes the march from intellect
through will to emotion as a progression of increasing concreteness (152). In the opening section of the chapter on the
emotions he attempts to say just what "the concrete" may be
(99-107). His account seems to be a fairly straightforward
appropriation of certain phenomenological themes commonly
associated with the name of Maurice Merleau-Ponty. [27] Its
first premise is a contrast between the testimony of the intellect and that of the emotions.

> Le connaître ... 'détache' l'objet, 'l'oppose' au
> moi; bref le connaître constitue la dualité du sujet
> et de l'objet (101).

It is conceptually difficult to suppose that the dualism indicated by the intellect can be the last word, and the emotions
attest that in point of fact it is not. The emotions bear witness to a participation "plus profonde que toute polarité et
que toute dualité" (101). Of this participation Ricoeur says:

> ... nous pouvons bien la nommer anté-prédicative,
> pré-réflexive, pré-objective, ou aussi bien hyper-
> prédicative, hyper-réflexive, hyper-objective (101).

And Ricoeur reaffirms his readiness to pursue this line of
thought to the very borders of ontology, if not through the
length and breadth of that domain (118-122). So it would
seem that Ricoeur has succeeded in sketching a way in which
the question of completeness, and beyond that the question of
grounding the subject-object relationship, might eventually be
resolved.

It comes as a surprise therefore when in a subsequent
passage Ricoeur sets out upon another line of response which
is quite distinct from the first and yet directed to the same
set of questions. Whereas the first type of response was
guided by the notion of the concrete, the second's identifying
theme is rather self-consciousness. [28] If the first paralleled
Merleau-Ponty, the second type of response bears resonances
of Hegel. Some time back we quoted from Ricoeur an observation about the mediating term as it operates on the level
of the intellect: emphasizing the entirely intentional character of the third term which mediates the "infinite" and "finite" poles, Ricoeur wrote that "l'étonnant est que ce troisi-
ème terme n'est pas donné en lui-même, mais seulement
dans la chose" (55). And again, in a similar vein: "cette
'conscience' n'est pas pour soi" (36, emphasis Ricoeur's).
In the context of the chapter on the emotions, these earlier
observations reappear substantially rephrased:

> ... le terme de la synthèse, celui que Kant appelle
> imagination transcendantale ... n'est nullement un
> vécu, une expérience susceptible d'être dramatisée
> ... (123)

Now we can assume that on each level the mediating term
stands pre-eminently for the human being (152). What has
been said of the third term may therefore be applied to the
human as well. Thus one can say that within the sphere of
the intellect "l'homme n'opère qu'en intention sa propre synthèse" (55). But Ricoeur has stipulated that a conscious

synthesis which is not self-conscious, which is not "conscience de soi," cannot be deemed genuinely human (55). Thus we arrive at a second sense of "incompleteness," a second sense in which the intellect proves in a fundamental way to be less than the entire self. Indeed the parallel with the discussion of concreteness may be extended one step further; for in this case as in the first it is the emotions which supply what is wanting:

> ... c'est le sentiment qui intériorise la raison; il me révèle que la raison est ma raison, car par lui je m'approprie la raison. (118, cf. 153)

This passage needs further attention and we shall return to it. For the moment it is enough to note that Ricoeur has succeeded in unearthing a second approach to the question of completeness. One need only recall the hegelian overtones of "self-consciousness" to suspect that he may have found a second response to the question of grounding as well.

As long as only one solution was in view, the question of grounding seemed on the verge of resolution. But two solutions are no solution at all as long as the relationship between them is uncertain. Once again the reader has in Ricoeur something which is either an embarrassment of riches or a confusion of categories. In either case the second solution, so far from securing matters, has recommitted our thought to flux.

It can be argued that we can regain firm ground if only we would give the lead to Ricoeur. After all, the two solutions are no more than ideal types constructed out of bits and pieces which were gathered, with little regard to context, out of the full range of L'homme faillible. Rather follow the train of Ricoeur's own exposition with an eye to sequence and purpose, and perhaps the tension between the types may prove to be no more than a function of their abstractness. Perhaps so. At the same time, however, we may hope that the types we have constructed will be of some use in illuminating the text. A typology which is woodenly conceived and mechanically applied is abusive, no doubt; but a text which is read uncritically is hardly better. Thus a good tactic may be not to start with the text cold, but to move toward it by a series of conceptual steps. The appropriateness of the steps will finally be judged by their helpfulness in reading the text; but the text, while it will furnish the final test, will not be the point from which we

depart. I shall rather begin by proposing at some length a
number of distinctions, first within the notion of the "concrete" and then within the notion of "self-consciousness. "
This will take time, because the issues are knotty in their
own right and because Ricoeur is often of little direct assistance. But if we do develop these distinctions to a point
where they may prove of use in an "explication de texte, "
then we may hope to enjoy Ricoeur's tacit support when, at
long last, we draw certain conclusions about the two types,
about the question of grounding and about the most basic
structure of L'homme faillible.

i. the "concrete": descriptive & metaphysical

       Ricoeur's proposal that the emotions be understood as
the privileged access to the concrete turns out to be one of
those gestures which simplifies a writing by immensely com-
plicating the work's interpretation. L'homme faillible is
given in a single stroke a coherence which had been belied
by the sequence of chapters with their distinct studies of the
intellect, the will and the emotions. It is a coherence which
had been obscured by the conventional interpretation as well;
for that reading has seemed unable to provide anything more
than a unity of theme, the formal unity bestowed by the recurrent structure of finite intuition and infinite intention.
When Ricoeur reveals that the incompleteness of the discussion of the intellect is the incompleteness not of a part but
of an abstraction, it is as if the entire work had suddenly
been telescoped into the one chapter on the "more concrete"
emotions!

       But telescoped into what, exactly? It is here that
the difficulties begin. For now the chapters themselves can
no longer be taken as so many tidy compartments bound
loosely by the recurrent paradigm. One may continue to
speak of levels within Ricoeur's study, and of levels of abstraction; but given that "level" necessarily connotes separation, the separateness of strata, one will precisely not speak
of levels within the human make-up. Ricoeur's proposal is
simple in the way in which a mathematical formula may be
elegant; and one may be forgiven for wishing on occasion
that the suggestion had never been made.

       But the proposal is not to be wished away or slighted.
It fits too well with Ricoeur's characteristic method. Specifically it fits the anti-reductionist resolution which we cited

at length a while back:

> Or si le progrès de la pensée, dans une anthro-
> pologie philosophique, ne consiste jamais à aller
> du simple au complexe, mais procède toujours à
> l'intérieur de la totalité même, ce ne peut être
> qu'un progrès dans l'élucidation philosophique de
> la vue globale. [29]

What is proposed is scarcely more than that this resolution
be taken in earnest. If indeed Ricoeur never proceeds from
the simple to the complex, it follows that he cannot have
taken the intellect as a preliminary part, much less as the
simplest part. And if his thinking always proceeds within
the totality it investigates, then the "pathétique de la 'misère'," while it is the fullest expression of that totality, is
not the only such expression. The discussion of the intellect too will be an expression of the totality, as an abstraction can be--and as a part cannot.

What then is Ricoeur's "concrete," that it can be the
unity to which the emotions witness and yet also be such that
the distinction of subject and object which is certified by the
intellect can be abstracted from it? It is this question, a
form of the venerable puzzle of the One and the Many, which
makes pertinent the distinction between a descriptive "concrete" and a prescriptive or metaphysical use of the term.

By the "descriptively" concrete I intend a use of the
term "concrete" which is restricted to the realm of actuali-
ties. It denotes therein the point or the case where several
sorts of actuality which have been previously discerned appear
to converge. Now I wish to suggest that the descriptively
concrete in L'homme faillible is not in fact the emotions, or
that to which the emotions alone bear witness, but rather
what Ricoeur calls "... la genèse réciproque du connaître et
du sentir..." (99, emphasis mine). The crucial passage
in this connection is placed at the beginning of the chapter
on the emotions, as if to set the context for that chapter;
and it is worth quoting in full:

> Replacés dans le mouvement de leur mutuelle pro-
> motion, sentir et connaître 's'expliquent' l'un par
> l'autre: d'un côté le pouvoir de connaître, en se
> hiérarchisant, engendre véritablement les degrés
> du sentiment et arrache ce dernier à son essen-
> tielle confusion; de l'autre le sentiment engendre

véritablement l'intention du connaître à tous ses
niveaux. C'est dans cette genèse mutuelle que
l'unité du sentir, du Fühlen, du feeling, se con-
stitue. [30]

The delineation of just what this may mean will have
to be tabled until we have drawn somewhat closer to Ricoeur's
text and can attempt a point-by-point reading of it. From
where we stand now, however, it is already possible, and
necessary, to make some general observations about the
function of the idea of "genèse réciproque" within the chapter
on the emotions. If the "genèse réciproque" is indeed the
descriptively concrete as I have suggested, it follows that it
is the closest approximation within the descriptive philosophic
context to the concrete totality originally evoked, in a pre-
philosophic context, by the quasi-poetic "pathétique de la
'misère'." Now one would suppose that the approximation
is the result of a process of approximating, the sort of
process indicated by Ricoeur when he says that the entirety
of L'homme faillible subsequent to the study of the intellect:

> ... consistera à combler progressivement cet
> écart entre le pathétique et le transcendantal, à
> récupérer philosophiquement toute la riche sub-
> stance qui ne passe pas dans la réflexion tran-
> scendantale appuyée sur l'objet (25).

And one would therefore expect that the "genèse réciproque"
would make its appearance at the end of the chapter on the
emotions, as the culmination of that final study.

In point of fact it comes up at the very beginning, as
we have remarked, and it is referred to consistently thereafter. In this placing of the concept we have a strong indication, though not yet proof, that between the "genèse réciproque" and the "pathétique de la 'misère'" there may be
not only a substantive correspondence but a formal correspondence as well. The "pathétique de la 'misère'" was
posed at the beginning of L'homme faillible; the subsequent
reflection which made up the body of the book was never
more than "un progrès dans l'élucidation philosophique" of
that given (24, emphasis Ricoeur's). Similarly I would suggest that the "genèse réciproque" is posed at the beginning
of the chapter on the emotions, and the remainder of the
chapter consists of elucidation.

At this point, however, one must exercise with

regard to the "genèse réciproque" the same caution which
Ricoeur urged in analogous circumstances with regard to "le
pathétique de la 'misère'": "il faut dissocier entièrement
l'idée de méthode en philosophie de celle de point de départ"
(24). One may have a pre-philosophic point of departure,
Ricoeur observes, and yet proceed in a manner which is perfectly philosophic (24). In the present case it is no less
true that one may start out from the descriptively concrete
and yet proceed in a manner which is not, itself, descriptive.
In short, "elucidation" is not necessarily description.

But a quick survey of the chapter on the emotions
would suggest that while the chapter is arranged somewhat
topically, its underlying logic remains descriptive not only
in its point of departure but in its development as well.
What the body of the chapter does in effect is to follow,
descriptively, the courses of two processes as they are generated by the "genèse réciproque." Indeed the processes are
the "genèse réciproque." They are specifically the processes
referred to in the long passage quoted earlier:

> ... d'un côté le pouvoir de connaître, en se hiér-
> archisant, engendre véritablement les degrés du
> sentiment ...; de l'autre le sentiment engendre
> véritablement l'intention du connaître à tous ses
> niveaux.[31]

Thus the distinction between philosophic method and point of
departure in L'homme faillible seems less extreme than one
might have supposed it to be, given the emphasis which Ricoeur himself puts upon it (24).

With our hypothesis regarding the "genèse réciproque"
in hand, we may turn at last to the second member of our
distinction, the prescriptively or metaphysically concrete.
Used prescriptively the term "concrete" claims to refer
beyond the realm of actuality. The manner of that real or
attempted extension will of course vary with certain metaphysical decisions; but in every case--we may stipulate--the
procedure will not be called simply descriptive. Description
is confined to actuality.

Now L'homme faillible does contain at least one important passage on the concept of being (118-122). But I
wish to suggest that the nature of Ricoeur's discussion is
such that he does not at any point opt for a particular metaphysical approach to being, or to the metaphysically concrete.

This suggestion would accord particular significance to the
fact that there are two sets of terminology within Ricoeur's
almost liturgical incantation, which we quoted earlier:

> nous pouvons bien la nommer anté-prédicative,
> pré-réflexive, pré-objective, ou aussi bien hyper-
> prédicative, hyper-réflexive, hyper-objective. [32]

The effect is that each set cancels the other as an indicator
of direction, i. e. as the emblem of a specific metaphysical
decision, so that there emerges from the clash no more than
the reference to an unspecified "beyond" (cf. 122). Put nega-
tively the suggestion is simply a corollary of the hypothesis
that Ricoeur's procedure is entirely descriptive. In a more
positive vein I would propose that the nature of Ricoeur's
discussions of the concept of being is that represented by his
dictum that "le sentiment atteste que, quel que soit l'être,
nous en sommes ... " (119, emphasis mine). The context in
which the dictum occurs, a contrasting of intellect and emotion, makes it clear that the thrust of "atteste" in this case
is experiential rather than logical. Thus the dictum is not
to be understood as propounding a thesis. It simply describes a conviction, a conviction occasioned by an experience,
direct or indirect, of the descriptively concrete. Of course
matters are complicated by the fact that the conviction happens to be about the metaphysically concrete. But even this
conviction does not pretend to be informative except in one
limited--and, as we shall soon see, peculiar--way. And in
any event the complication can hardly alter the nature of the
dictum as description. I would argue that something similar
holds true of all of Ricoeur's apparent forays into the realm
of ontology in the course of L'homme faillible.

To summarize our discussion of the "concrete": we
distinguished on the one hand the "descriptively concrete";
and it was suggested that in L'homme faillible the descriptively concrete is not emotion per se but the interaction of
emotion and intellect, the "genèse réciproque," which concept was introduced for the first time on this occasion. On
the other hand we distinguished the "prescriptively concrete,"
which we also called the "metaphysical concrete"; and this
leg of the distinction like the first was accompanied by a
proposal. It was suggested that strictly speaking the prescriptively concrete does not enter into the structure of
L'homme faillible. On several occasions it is referred to;
but always and only as "beyond." Within the conceptual
structure which is proper to L'homme faillible, the concrete

is the descriptively concrete and the descriptively concrete
is the concrete.

ii.   "self-consciousness" & the paradox of the emotions

      We turn now to Ricoeur's second type of response to
the problem of grounding, the problem of the relationship between intellect and emotion.   This is the response rooted in
the concept of "self-consciousness. "

      With the change of topic we confront a second blind-
spot afflicting the conventional reading of L'homme faillible.
For the reading which slights the problems involved in saying
that emotion gives access to the concrete is also overly sanguine about the implications of saying that emotion is intentional.   This handicap is felt the moment one takes seriously
what Ricoeur has called "le paradoxe du sentiment" (101, emphasis mine).   "Le sentiment ... est sans aucun doute intentionnel: il est un sentir 'quelque chose' ... " (100).   But,
he goes on to say:

          ... c'est une intentionnalité bien étrange, que
          d'une part désigne des qualités senties sur les
          choses, sur les personnes, sur le monde, d'autre
          part manifeste, révèle la manière dont le moi est
          intimement affecté (100).

Given the statement that the emotions are intentional, the
conventional interpretation fastens hard upon the implication
that emotional experience possesses a structure and that it
is therefore not ineffable.   It can be talked about.   That interpretation stresses moreover that the structure is closely
analogous to the structure which was successfully delineated
in Ricoeur's discussion of intellectual experience; and from
this it draws the further conclusion that emotional experience
can be talked about in detail.   All of this is true enough.
But to leave matters at this point, as the interpretation commonly does, is to stop short of ever raising the crucial
question of what is specific to the emotions.   On that question, the intentional structure is only a preliminary help; and
in the end it may prove an outright obstacle.   This ominous
possibility will be the burden of much of what is to follow.

      The implication of Ricoeur's paradox is that emotion
is somehow "between" the object and the self, and intimately
bound to each.   This is putting matters rather graphically

perhaps, but hardly any more so than Ricoeur's own remark
that "par eux-mêmes l'aimable et le haïssable ne sont que
des épithètes flottantes ... " (100). Now if we follow the
image of emotion as "between" the object and the self, we
find that Ricoeur's immediate discussion of the paradox
treats only the first of the relationships, that between emotion and object (100-101). Ricoeur carefully notes that the
experienced qualities are bound intimately to their objects:
they are "on" the objects, "sur les choses." Yet they are
distinct from their objects, "... le moment d'extériorité ne
leur appartient pas ... " (100). But no comparable attention
is given to the relationship between emotion and the self.
Ricoeur himself is content with the sort of convenient omis-
sion which one would associate with the conventional view.

     The omission may tacitly reflect how difficult it is to
come at the relationship from the side of the self. For ap-
proached from the side of the object-emotion relationship,
the paradox of the emotions still seems no more than what
we may call a paradox of fact. It is odd that matters as
different in their natures as intentional object and emotion
should happen, in the performance, to be so closely juxta-
posed; but it is no more than an odd fact. If, on the other
hand, one insists upon approaching matters from the emotion-
self side, there is revealed not the same paradox in another
aspect but a paradox of another sort altogether. For as regards the self, the paradox of the emotions is what one
would have to call a conceptual paradox in contrast to the
paradox of fact.

     In a paradox of fact the members appear together but
may be conceived of as existing apart; and each member so
conceived retains a certain content. Thus there is a certain
content to hatefulness apart from the object hated; and the
common sense conviction that there is a content to the object
apart from emotion and the like is of course the perennial
root of the notion of primary qualities. But in the conceptual paradox, as I propose the term be understood, the two
elements must in principle be said to be distinct--and yet
one of the two is such that apart from its alliance with the
other it cannot be conceived. Or in so far as it is so conceived, the concept proves to be totally lacking in content;
which may be to say that strictly speaking it is not conceived, but simply posited.

     I am suggesting that as regards the self, Ricoeur's
paradox of the emotions is a conceptual paradox. If a

stranger were to inquire about a particular person, he would
probably be told something about the person's relationships,
the common sort of data that one gets; he would be introduced, in effect, to the subject as object.   If that should not
be enough and the stranger were to inquire further, he might
begin to construct careful imaginative accounts of the subject's experience, the likely experiences of the intentional
subject; thus for example a biographer might write, "How
strange it all must have seemed to him that September morn-
ing as he stood at the door of his new home. " But such experiences are still relationships; and the point which I am
concerned to make is that if for some extraordinary reason
the stranger should take it into his head to press even beyond
them, then the most that he could do would be to posit a re-
ceding point, a shrinking sphere of that which is most strictly the subject's own or of that to which the subject most
strictly belongs. 33   This point at the furthest boundary of
the intentional subject is the limit-idea of the isolated self.
Perhaps we may put the matter in terms of linguistics as
well.   To call something one's own, for example, is to use
a relational term.   But it would seem that to each relationship there is contributed something which has no proper content apart from the relationship and other relationships like
it, but which is not reducible to the relationship nor even to
the sum of all the relationships which might be pertinent.

        It is this conceptual paradox, I would suggest, which
gives the paradox of the emotions its bite.   We may appreciate its role if we look again at Ricoeur's formulation.   Ricoeur says that the intentionality of the emotions is "une intentionnalité bien étrange" (100); but as he formulates it the
paradox is prima facie a paradox of fact:

            ... c'est une intentionnalité ..., qui d'une part
            désigne des qualités senties sur les choses, sur
            les personnes, sur le monde, d'autre part mani-
            feste, révèle la manière dont le moi est ... af-
            fecté (100, emphasis Ricoeur's).

That is, the paradox seems to lie in the juxtaposing or con-
flating of an intention and a relation.   One's relationship to
an object ("la manière dont le moi est ... affecté") is experienced on the object ("sur les choses").   But this is not
the full thrust of the paradox, even as Ricoeur himself would
have it.   Ricoeur supplies one further term which we deleted
a moment ago: he speaks of "la manière dont le moi est
intimement affecté. "34   This evocation of a subjective inte-

rior is precisely a reference to the conceptual paradox. And
it is experiencing that--the elusive interior suddenly con-
fronted "sur les choses"--which makes of emotion an intentionality so very "bien étrange. "

Of course none of this is meant as a resolution of the
conceptual paradox. Quite the contrary, it is offered as evidence that the paradox is indeed well founded. And confirmation of good rootage is just the thing we need in order to
build upon the paradox a further step, a distinction within
our notion of "self-consciousness. " To begin with the given
object, in good ricoeurian fashion, we may recall that there
is, on the one hand, an intentional self-consciousness. This
is simply the phenomenon which we have already observed
at the emotional paradox's common, unreflective periphery:
one is indirectly aware of oneself, i. e. one is indirectly
aware of one's emotional state while being (directly) aware
of the object as it is experienced. But our study of the
paradox suggests as well that one might also posit the concept of an isolated self-consciousness. This would be an
awareness of that sphere which is properly one's own or to
which one most properly belongs.

Speaking quite strictly one would have to say that an
isolated self-consciousness is, like its object the isolated
self, a limit-idea. But one speaks strictly only when one is
driven to it. Common usage is quite rightly content to do
commerce among a number of spheres, all of which are
more or less one's own. To pursue the metaphor, it is
enough for everyday usage that the spheres be roughly con-
centric. The center itself is a matter of speculation.

The objection may be raised that to offer this everyday usage as an example of isolated self-consciousness is no
more than sleight-of-hand. The case is in fact the very opposite of what we have said. For surely one claims something as one's own--so that if there is self-consciousness
here at all, it must be intentional. We may reply that the
objection is entirely right in what it affirms but wrong in
what it would deny. Actually the case is both, an instance
of intentional self-consciousness and an instance of isolated
self-consciousness as well; and either aspect may be high-
lighted depending upon the frame of reference. Take for example the case of my calling something my own. First compare that to the case of my simply calling something mine.
The emphasis falls upon my having something my own and
the self-consciousness seems isolated. Then compare it to

my speaking of my self. The emphasis shifts to my having
called some thing my own and the self-consciousness appears
intentional.

All this is simply to say that a relatively isolated
self-consciousness is isolated only relatively and that to the
extent that the self-consciousness is not one thing, namely
isolated, it is the other, namely intentional. The objection
and the response have been of help, however, in bringing
more fully to light the fact that throughout our discussion of
self-consciousness, of the subject or self, and of that which
is one's own, there have recurred certain characteristics
which are peculiar to limit-ideas. In particular, the bounds
of each of the concepts which we have touched upon possesses an odd tendency to "slide. " By this I mean something
more than that the boundaries are simply vague. For it is
not that there is simply a grey middle ground lying between
two realms which themselves are fixed and clear. It is
rather that the entire terrain may be occupied by the one
camp at one moment and by the other at another. This
capacity to be everywhere and nowhere would seem to lie in
the very nature of a limit-idea, which has no content in its
own right but which is capable of the most encompassing in-
stantiations; and we may attribute the capacity most especially to the limit-idea of "belonging"--the concept of that which
is one's own or of that to which one belongs--which appears
to be at the root of the other limit-ideas of self and of self-
consciousness.

What is impressive in these waxings and wanings is
the sheer tenacity with which some form of the limit-idea of
belonging is consistently retained. The concept refuses even
at the moment of its greatest extension to be resolved into
elements more simple than itself. And it cannot ever be
dispensed with, even when it has contracted to a point. It
is for this reason that I would propose that the concept of
belonging be understood as a category. This is to say simply that it is a concept which is indispensable for some pur-
pose--in this case, for the describing of the fullness of
human experience--and that it is irreducible.

It is also a concept which requires a foil. The exact
sense of a concept of that which is not one's own or of that
to which one does not belong need not detain us; we may
speak in common sense terms of "neutrality" and "objectivity. " The next section will refine this characterization a bit,
but pressing for a full definition of "objectivity" would march

us into philosophy of science and away from our primary purpose. [35] More important to that purpose is the implication
that if "belonging" is a category, then the same must be true
of the partner-concept as well, however it be defined. It is
important because with the appearance of the second category
we at last have the makings of a duality which is intrinstic
to L'homme faillible and which yet corresponds to the duality
of languages in the thought of Gabriel Marcel.

II. THE FRAMEWORKS:
Their assets & limitations

We began our effort to understand L'homme faillible
by setting forth its conventional interpretation. With an eye
toward the shape of the book's Table of Contents we may call
that interpretation the "horizontal" view, since the framework
upon which it is based is contained within each successive
chapter and does not appear to concern itself with the relationship between the several chapters or levels. The next
phase of our study grew out of a criticism of the horizontal
interpretation; but it soon became apparent that it would be
no easy matter to frame a coherent alternative. The "vertical" relationship between intellect and emotion was ambiguous at best, and our long venture into distinction-making
has been simply an effort to get that relationship clear. [36]

A logical next step would be to test whether the distinctions have succeeded in their intent and then, if it seems
that they have, to propose a vertical perspective as a supplement to the conventional interpretation or as a replace-
ment of it. I wish to argue, however, that the distinctions
which we have made can do more than clarify the vertical
relations and commend an alternative reading of L'homme
faillible, though they can do that as well. They make it possible, I believe, to tackle the second-order question of the
relation between the relations, vertical and horizontal, and
thus they enable the reader to embrace the entire work within an integrative view.

As a first move toward such integration it might be
useful if we were to try not simply to demonstrate but to
delineate the precise inadequacies of each of the presently
conspicuous aspirants to the role of fundamental framework
in L'homme faillible. The delineation may serve as a device
by which the distinctions prepared for the earlier, preliminary task of shaping a vertical interpretation to match the

horizontal can be commandeered for the present task of attaining an integrative view.   For I anticipate that the delineation will reveal the features of a certain ambiguity inherent
to the structure of L'homme faillible; and I wish to argue
that so long as this ambiguity is overlooked, the reader will
be helpless to prevent the cardinal polarities from merging
and dividing among themselves at whim.   But once that ambiguity has been nailed, the truly fundamental framework is
virtually in hand.

We may begin by sketching somewhat more systematically a few criteria which should hold good for whatever
framework is to be considered most basic to L'homme faillible.   Two which come immediately to mind are analytically
true and would hold for any work: the fundamental framework
will not be reducible to any other framework; and it will be
seen in some sense to underlie whatever other frameworks
there may be--not that all can be smartly collapsed into the
one (Ricoeur's thought is not so deductive as that) but that
at the least the rest can be importantly related to the one.

So much is obvious.   In addition, however, I would
propose one further criterion: the elements of that framework which is fundamental to L'homme faillible will be uneasy with one another; between them there will be continual
conflict.   Now this tension cannot help but call to mind the
marcellian duality of language; and as we said at the outset,
that duality must be ruled out of court as an extrinsic consideration until it has been proved otherwise.   So if our
study is to be pursuasive we need to show that this third
criterion can be erected on grounds which are intrinsic to
L'homme faillible.   A good springboard to that demonstration is Ricoeur's remark that:

> Seul en effet le sentiment peut révêler la fragilité
> comme conflit; sa fonction d'intériorisation, in-
> verse de celle de l'objectivation du connaître, ex-
> plique que la même dualité humaine qui se projette
> dans la synthèse de l'objet se réflêchisse en con-
> flit (122-3, emphasis Ricoeur's).

On Ricoeur's premises this vision of conflict must be regarded as touching upon the fundamentals of human nature--
as revealing "la même dualité" more truly--because it remains the peculiar though still unexplained privilege of the
emotions to give access to the fundamental, to the "concrete."
Ricoeur's introduction of the conflict, however, is only the

long-delayed accomplishment of a task which had been inte-
gral to his work from the beginning.   It is in fact the task
which defines L'homme faillible in its relation to La symbolique du mal: namely the task of making a philosophic approach to the mystery of evil before the fact by delineating
what we have called the frailty of man.   The pre-philosophic
measure of that approach is "le pathétique de la 'misère'."[37]
But the gap was extreme between the "pathétique" on the one
hand and, on the other hand, the initial "disproportion"
treated in the discussion of the intellect.   Therefore the
work's own logic would require that intellectual "disproportion" give way to emotional "conflict" in order that, at one
and the same time, the possibility of evil be adumbrated and
that which is most fundamental to the human be attained.

Assuming three criteria then and taking the two conspicuous candidates seriatim (first the finite/infinite polarity
and then the polarity of intellect and emotion), we have a
rough outline upon which to proceed.

a.   the finite/infinite framework

Irreducibility is the first claimant's forte.   The compelling character of the horizontal view arises in large part
from the sense that with the concepts of "finite" and "infinite" one has touched bottom at last.   There is truth to
this, but it is a truth which is better put by saying one has
finally reached the ceiling; for these concepts are not so
much irreducible as unsubsumable.   Their strength is in
their generality; and we have already had indications that
therein may lie a weakness as well.[38]

The horizontal reading of L'homme faillible is virtually defined by the assumption that for a set of concepts to
have been recurrent is in some sense for them to have become comprehensive as well.   We have seen that the second
test is not to be passed so easily, however; for if the concepts can only slice one way, there is no way in which fre-
quency can endow them with comprehensiveness.   And if in
addition the concepts are of a very general sort, then it is
all the less likely that they will prove sufficiently rich to
pull together the entirety of a work.   This is in effect the
conclusion we reached some time ago when, prompted by the
observation that "finite" and "infinite" cannot be ranged along
the vertical axis, we set out in quest of something more
satisfying than the conventional view.[43]   We observed at that

time that this shortcoming may be the obverse of another of
Ricoeur's treatment's peculiar strengths--namely its insistence that "il faut entièrement renoncer à l'idée de lier le
fini à une faculté ou fonction et l'infini à une autre faculté
ou fonction" (22).   Since then we have been giving the vertical axis a closer inspection and our initial assessment would
seem to have been confirmed.   At least one characteristic
which is specific to the emotions, and which thus helps define the nature of the axis, namely the factor of self-consciousness, simply finds no place within the framework of
the finite and infinite.

          With the third test we have our first brush with Ri-
coeur's structural ambiguity.   It is clear that one instance
of the finite/infinite polarity does issue in conflict.   That
was the point of the passage on the emotions which we quoted
a moment ago, ("Seul en effet le sentiment peut révéler la
fragilité comme conflit . . . ," 122-3); and the passage is borne
out in the prime example of conflict within the emotions,
namely the tension between pleasure and happiness, which
Ricoeur seems indeed to define as a conflict between specific instances of the finite and infinite (109).   But if one
turns from the level of the emotions to the level of the in-
tellect--which level, if more abstract, is also avowedly the
clearer indicator of the polarity's nature--one finds that the
poles are remarkably amicable, resting calmly in the synthesis of "l'imagination pure"; and the effect of this counter-
example is to make it unlikely that the conflict which does
emerge at the level of the emotions can be attributed to the
finite/infinite polarity per se.   The accomplishment which
inadvertently occasioned this limitation was Ricoeur's ingen-
ious mating of the finite/infinite polarity with the polarity of
intuition and empty intention.   As we noted at the time, the
effect of that marriage was to check the drift of the finite/
infinite distinction toward dualism. [40]   Now we find that finite
intuition and infinite intention have become so thoroughly correlative that while through their generality they may perhaps
encompass conflict, they are unable through their nature
specifically to account for it.

b.   the intellect/emotion framework

          If we turn now to the intellectual/emotional polarity
and raise the question of reducibility, Ricoeur's structural
ambiguity pushes abruptly to the foreground.   It is basic to
Ricoeur's system that intellect and emotion each consist of a

a specific interplay of finite and infinite factors.   Might it
not follow then that the polarity itself, the distinction between
intellect and emotion, is a function of a preponderance of the
infinite factor in the one case and a preponderance of the
finite factor in the other?   The suggestion is in flagrant defi-
ance of Ricoeur's solemn strictures against the equating of
finitude and infinitude with specific faculties or functions ("Il
faut entièrement renoncer à l'idée ...," 22)--and yet it seems
undeniable that there is a sense in which emotion is like Ricoeur's "finite," if only the finite be understood in conjunction
with intuition as he himself suggests; and there is a sense in
which the intellect is like Ricoeur's "infinite," when the infinite is taken in tandem with empty intentionality.   This, I
wish to suggest, is the sort of ambiguity which makes
L'homme faillible so rich and so exasperating a work, and
which makes necessary the lengths to which our own discussion has gone.   The present stand-off between Ricoeur's
prohibition and our own suspicions is the furthest point
reached to date in our effort to pin that ambiguity down.

        It must be acknowledged, however, that our ability to
apply the criterion of comprehensiveness can be no more
definite than our sense of the system's structure; and the
discovery of ambiguity has rendered that quite shaky.   We
can only say with regard to the second test that insofar as
the two approaches remain mutually exclusive, the vertical
approach is unlikely to succeed at a task at which the horizontal has already failed.   But if the axes were to merge,
anything is possible.

        Irreducibility was the first polarity's forte, a point
of clear superiority over the alternative.   Similarly the in-
tellectual/emotional polarity has in the third criterion, the
ability to account for the presence of conflict within the human self, an arena of clear and characteristic advantage.
In making this claim, I have no intention of slighting the
several passages in which Ricoeur ascribes the actuality of
conflict to the finite/infinite structure (107ff.).   That is indeed the shape which the conflict takes.   But we have seen
that other cases take that shape as well and conflict does
not occur. [41]   On Ricoeur's own account the crucial factor
is the presence of emotion and especially of emotional self-
awareness (107ff.); and thus the crucial factor is somehow
allied with the distinctions contained within the vertical axis.
This is not necessarily to say that the conflict is between
the poles of that axis.   It is to say that in explaining conflict the presence of the axis, in part or in toto, will be an
important consideration.

This concludes our summation of the strengths and
weaknesses of the major polarities as explanatory frameworks.
The liabilities brought to light make clear that neither candi-
date can of itself account for what is most basic to the human
nature depicted in L'homme faillible. This conclusion heightens the significance of a phenomenon which until now has been
at the periphery of our attention, namely the apparent ambiguity in the structure of L'homme faillible. First, our conclusion gives evidence that the ambiguity is more than apparent;
for the ambiguity amounts to an insistence that the two frameworks are not ultimate, and that proposal has been borne out.
Further, our conclusion reinforces the question with which
our study of L'homme faillible began, namely the question of
what is fundamental to this anthropology; and the structural
ambiguity emerges as our last, best clue to a response. By
the very fact that it casts doubt upon the ultimacy of the distinction between the two polarities, the ambiguity presses the
question of their interrelationship and points us beyond. The
final section of our study of L'homme faillible will follow out
this lead.

III. EXPLICATION DE TEXTE:
The structural ambiguity of L'homme faillible

Our study thus far has amounted to an extended pref-
ace, preparing the way for the exposition of a particular
text.[42] To ready us to penetrate the surface of the text,
that surface had to be rendered problematic. So we have
been turning up questions. But a problem well posed is in
a good way toward being resolved, and each question has
sharpened the question which had preceded it. Thus the question of grounding subject and object was a partial and preliminary putting of the recent question of the relationship between
the major frameworks; and the appearance of a structural ambiguity confirmed that this relationship between the frameworks
is not an idle question but an issue of some urgency. It is
encouraging to reflect that matters which have been so interdependent in the asking may be interdependent in their resolution as well. If one is toppled, others may follow.

Thematically, Ricoeur's chapter on the emotions, "La
fragilité affective," is, as the title suggests, the culmination
of his progressive delineation of human "frailty."[43] And in
ways which have yet to be fully defined, this chapter is the
part which somehow gives access to the whole; pars pro toto,
the emotions are the locus of self-consciousness and the
means of access to the concrete. Let us start then by apply-

ing to the part the question we once asked with regard to the whole, "What is the basic conceptual framework which obtains here?" And once again let us start by briefly examining the author's own pronouncements. We may focus upon the second section, pages 107-122, which in many ways is the most crucial portion of the chapter. Even within this one section there is a variety of statement. In the opening paragraph Ricoeur lays down the thesis that "la disproportion du connaître puisse à la fois se refléter et s'achever dans celle du sentiment" (107). The passage could be a locus classicus for the horizontal reading of L'homme faillible: it holds that the conceptual framework developed in the study of the intellect is simply to be extended to the will and to the emotions. The same might be said of the lines shortly thereafter which enunciate, in Ricoeur's words, the "central theme" of the entire discussion:

> ... à savoir que le sentir se dédouble comme le connaître, proportionnellement au connaître et pourtant autrement que le connaître, sur un mode non objectif, sur le mode du conflit intérieur.
> (107, emphases Ricoeur's)

Everything depends upon the weight one assigns to the "autrement." In any event the case for the horizontal reading of the section would seem to be secured by the subsequent passage in which Ricoeur links the two cardinal terms of the horizontal axis to the two cardinal terms of the present section. "Pleasure" is explicitly linked to finitude; and Ricoeur implicitly associates "happiness" with the infinite or indefinite, which he calls "l'oeuvre totale de l'homme" (109).

In point of fact, however, this seemingly definitive passage and its implementation are sandwiched between other passages which invoke a very different framework. Most striking is the detailed statement on the previous page:

> ... toute notre réflexion sur la disproportion vient donc se concentrer en un point, qui est en quelque sorte le lieu et le noeud de la disproportion; c'est ce noeud affectif que Platon appela 'thumos' et qu'il chercha à situer entre l''epithumia,' le désir sensible, et la raison dont l''eros' est par ailleurs le désir spécifique. C'est donc dans le 'thumos' que s'aiguise le conflit intime à la désirabilité humaine ... [44]

We may be fairly confident that Ricoeur is speaking once
again of "pleasure" and "happiness," the two specific forms
of desire. But what he is saying about them seems suddenly
quite different. Whatever the final word about this passage
may be--and we will have to ask whether "la raison" is exactly the same as intellect, and whether the "sensible" is
exactly emotion--one's first observation must be that it suggests the vertical axis far more than it does the horizontal.
Thus Ricoeur's own statements with regard to framework are
rather mixed.

This indecision in Ricoeur's opening pronouncements
is mirrored in the execution. The entire chapter on the
emotions fluctuates between the horizontal and vertical frameworks. In his first section Ricoeur uses the vertical framework (99-107); with the beginning of the second section he
shifts to the horizontal (107f.) and that perspective rules almost exclusively until page 118. At that point the vertical
framework is reintroduced and thereafter the exposition is
mixed in the most telling way. For the moment however I
simply wish to call attention to an inconspicuous point of
transition at the foot of page 118, nestled between two sentences:

> D'une côté c'est la raison, en tant qu'ouverture sur
> la totalité, qui engendre le sentiment, en tant
> qu'ouverture sur le bonheur. En retour c'est le
> sentiment qui intériorise la raison; il me révèle
> que la raison est ma raison, car par lui je m'ap-
> proprie la raison.

Radiating outward from this point is a rather lovely symmetry,
the more significant if it should be inadvertent, which tends to
confirm that this unprepossessing point is indeed the hinge of
something important. First and most obviously there are the
two sentences themselves, which recall the two opposite and
complementary sides of the "genèse réciproque" (cf. 99).
Then at a distance of one paragraph in either direction Ricoeur quotes and quotes again a certain "beau texte" from
Kant, but with opposite and complementary emphases. And
finally, further still in each direction lie passages in which
Ricoeur introduces certain important concepts ("la raison" in
the one case, p. 118, and "l'appartenance" in the other,
p. 119) which concepts, I shall argue, are also opposite and
complementary.

So there is stylistic evidence, at least, that our two

conceptual frameworks are indigenous to Ricoeur's chapter on
the emotions. The further question is whether the chapter
also reflects the structural ambiguity which seems to obtain
between the conceptual frameworks. This question has to be
answered in roundabout fashion, but the reward of patience
is a prize example of the ambiguity. Let us begin with an
unambiguous case; then let us pursue it and see whether it
turns into its opposite. The pursuit will proceed in two
steps, by way of two crucial passages.

The first step may be introduced by observing that the
very heart of what I have called the unambiguously horizontal
portion of the chapter's second section (viz 109-118) is the
premise that "happiness" represents a perspective which is
more encompassing than is that of "pleasure" (e. g. 109).
More specifically, it is understood that happiness bespeaks
a vista which is in principle aperspectival, unbounded by a
finite perspective, and which therefore subsumes the finite
ends of pleasure, though without negating those ends (e. g.
110). Ricoeur's line of thought here is of course an elaborate parallel of his earlier dialectic of perspective and word
on the level of the intellect; and one naturally assumes that
it is all meant on analogy with the intellect (cf. "comme le
connaître," p. 107), but on analogy only (cf. "pourtant autrement," p. 107). This horizontal interpretation is shaken,
however, when Ricoeur announces that:

> ... ce qui dans la confusion affective distingue la
> visée du bonheur de la visée du plaisir c'est la
> raison, la raison au sens kantien, la raison en
> tant qu'exigence de la totalité; le bonheur est de
> même amplitude que la raison; nous sommes
> capables de bonheur, parce que la raison 'demande
> la totalité absolue des conditions pour une condition
> donnée' (Dialectique de la Raison pratique, début).
> (118)

With this passage the entire landscape seems to have shifted.
No longer do we simply have a relationship between pleasure
and happiness within the sphere of the emotions. Rather, it
now appears that the sphere of the intellect is somehow subsuming the entirety of emotion, including pleasure and happiness alike. It follows that the relationship between the
spheres or levels of Ricoeur's study is no longer simply one
of analogy; it is no longer simply one in which the finite element on one level corresponds to the finite element on another level, and so on. Rather, the relationship is concentrated

at one end of the common polarity, at the pole of infinitude; and at that point the relationship seems to be one of virtual identity. Finally, this remarkable passage claims to be telling us what has been going on throughout the course of the pleasure/happiness dialectic. If the ambiguity is indeed manifest here, it must have been latent throughout the preceding ten pages.

There is one reassuring argument. After all, to think that the ambiguity is upon us assumes the synonymity of "intellect" and "reason" in Ricoeur. "Intellect" is the word which we accepted faute de mieux as a translation of "le connaître," a sphere comprising both finite perception and certain infinite capacities of language. [45] Of "reason" we know a great deal less: only that Ricoeur proposes it as a factor common to both intellect and emotion, represented therein by the capacities for language and for happiness respectively; and that it is presumably responsible for the peculiarly "infinite" character of these capacities, since it somehow acts as an "exigence de la totalité" (118). Thus in what we know of Ricoeur's use of the terms there is no necessity to consider the two as one, and there may be some good reasons not to. If the terms are kept distinct, so the argument concludes, the relationship of simple analogy is preserved.

It is preserved indeed--until Ricoeur's next passage and our second step. The passage occurs on the same page as the one we have just dealt with; and indeed it is in the same context, for Ricoeur has just been quoting Kant on the role of reason. He then observes:

> Ce texte fait bien entendre ce que peut signifier une genèse réciproque de la raison et du senti-ment. (118, emphasis mine)

Now on the basis of the argument of a moment ago one could have understood an interaction between reason and pleasure, for that would be an interaction within the sphere of emotion or "sentiment." But this passage and its subsequent restatements (118) speak of an interaction between reason and an entire sphere or level; and that usage must reawaken the suspicion that after all there is some sense in which reason is not simply a factor which happens to be common to several spheres or levels, but is itself a sphere or level--which could hardly be other than that of the intellect. The suspicion is strengthened when one reflects that "genèse récipro-

que" is something of a technical term in Ricoeur, so that he
would not have used it lightly (99). And it is further en-
couraged when one considers the importance of this passage,
and the role of the "genèse réciproque" more generally, in
the stylistic structure of the present chapter. For this is
precisely the passage which is, as I have begun to argue,
the pivot between two important portions of Ricoeur's second
section, and thus by implication the summary of the one and
the announcement of the other;[46] in a very real sense the
"genèse réciproque" is the foundation which underlies the
chapter as a whole (99f., 107f.). The final confirmation of
our suspicion comes when we check back to the earlier appearances of the "genèse" and discover that in each case Ricoeur describes an interaction which is for the most part
identical to that set forth on page 118 (99f., 107f.); that in
one case he expressly calls this "la genèse réciproque" (99);
and that in sum there is hardly any major difference between
the three accounts--except that on pages 99 and 107 Ricoeur
speaks consistently of an interaction of "le sentiment" and
"le connaître" (emphasis mine).

        The conclusion to be drawn is not that "reason" and
"intellect" are synonymous after all. Indeed if it were, the
relationship between the terms and between the frameworks
would not be so ambiguous. The implication is rather that
there is some sense, and that there are certain moments, in
which the two terms can be functionally equivalent. To put
the matter more comprehensively: reason can take the part
of the idea of happiness, interacting with pleasure (or indeed
the part of language interacting with visual perspective), and
it can take the part of the entire sphere of the intellect interacting with the sphere of the emotions; and in some unexplained manner it can take all these parts at once. That
these very different interactions can so blend into one another
--and perhaps, at bottom, it is simply this capacity which
the term "reason" represents--constitutes the clearest instance of what I have referred to as Ricoeur's structural ambiguity.

        I have been at pains to delineate this ambiguity, first
in the abstract[47] and now in a specific instance, because it
is the major obstacle in the way of a systematic understanding of L'homme faillible, and at the same time the major in-
centive to an integrative view. Were it not for this ambiguity one could rest content with saying that there are two perspectives, each of which throws a partial light on L'homme
faillible. But with the ambiguity before us it becomes evident

that in a sense there are not two distinct frameworks, and
the question of what there is becomes urgent. The relation
between the frameworks ceases to be a matter of casual
speculation and becomes a pressing issue.

As a final stage preparatory to drawing conclusions
about that issue, I propose to shift the mode of our "explanation." Throughout the present section we have tried
simply to listen to the text, confining ourselves to general,
"naïve" questions. The section has been lengthy because our
method has necessarily tended toward that of a cumulative
word study. I propose that we now shift to a more categorical approach. We shall distinguish in the text the operation
of the two conceptual frameworks and we shall then summarize briefly the contrasting ways in which the two points
of view lead one to interpret a certain sequence of topics,
namely Ricoeur's concepts of "thumos," of the infinite, of
human frailty and of self-consciousness. If these summaries
can give us some synoptic view of how the frameworks actually function, we may be in a better position to say how
they are related.

a.   the finite/infinite framework in operation

As its title indicated, the first section of Ricoeur's
chapter on the emotions dealt briefly with "intentionnalité et
intimité," the two facets of the paradox which is endemic to
the emotions (99-107). Of these two aspects it is clearly
"intentionality" which Ricoeur has chosen to elaborate upon
at the beginning of the subsequent section (109f.). He has
already established in the course of an earlier skirmish with
behaviorism that the emotions do possess an intentionality of
their own (102) and he indeed announced at that time that
this proposition would form "la pierre angulaire de toute
notre réflexion" (102). Accordingly, when he says that his
method will be to examine "les affections qui terminent le
mouvement du besoin, de l'amour, du désir," (109, emphasis
Ricoeur's) the reader may understand that his method will be
to examine the emotions which most clearly manifest the intentional object; and the reader may suppose that "pleasure"
and "happiness" are selected with this end in view. That
such is indeed Ricoeur's program is suggested in the following paragraph when Ricoeur speaks of happiness as "l'autre
visée affective," along with pleasure (109, emphasis mine).
But the crucial confirmation that Ricoeur does intend to proceed by referring to the intentional objects comes when, in

order to bring home the crucial distinction between happiness and pleasure, Ricoeur at last introduces the long-post-
poned topic of the hierarchy of possible objects (113, cf. 99-
100, 107). Under the impact of this crucial move, pages
109-118 become in essence a study of the unsettling and finally controlling effect which a larger and indeed infinite empty
intention can have upon a lesser, fulfilled intention.

   These reflections are enough to secure two points or
observations which might occur to any reader. The first is
simply that we have here a study of intentionality and specifically a study of certain types of intentionality, a typology.
Thus the pages are virtually a pure case of the horizontal
perspective and offer a convenient reference point for our
study of the operations of that framework. The second point
concerns a certain rationalist bent to Ricoeur's present argument. By this I mean simply that the sole dynamic of the
argument seems to be a constant logical pressure exerted by
an empty intention in the direction of an ever more comprehensive context. It becomes increasingly evident that Ricoeur
has placed some sort of premium upon the infinite side of
his polarity; and it becomes increasingly difficult to know
what positive significance could attach to the finite elements
in their own right, apart from their role as steps toward the
larger whole, or as elements in it. 48 In our "Conclusion"
we will want to look critically at this weighting of Ricoeur's
polarity; and we will want to ask whether that bias, if bias
it be, is not inherent in the horizontal approach. For the
moment however we may content ourselves with a brief indication of the ways that rationalist setting affects certain concepts which are crucial to Ricoeur's understanding of the
emotions.

   Ricoeur speaks repeatedly of a third, mediating term
within the polarity of the emotions; and for this term, which
will be the seat of the intensest human fragility, he proposes
the name of "heart" or "thumos" (98, 122). Now let us try
to create an ideal type by embracing without reservation the
rationalist tendency and then reasoning deductively from that
rationalism as a first principle. How then will we conceive
of the mediating term? Clearly, it will mediate in the specific sense of being transitional, a transition toward a higher,
more rational point from a point which is inferior. We may
further postulate that the restlessness of the emotions will be
explained by reference to the ever more encompassing demands
of this higher point, of the infinite pole; and the fragility of
one's emotional nature will be ascribed to the clashing of

these demands with the recalcitrance or inertia of the lower, finite pole. Finally, on these rationalist premises "self-consciousness" would clearly be aligned in some way with the higher or infinite pole.

Surprisingly enough a number of Ricoeur's passages do bear at least a family resemblance to the type we have constructed. The interpretation of the mediating term as transitional is explicit in the opening pages of the chapter, when Ricoeur introduces "thumos" as "la transition vivante du 'bios' au 'logos'" (98). The ascription of the restlessness of the emotions to the workings of the infinite pole is apparent in an important polemical passage in which Ricoeur argues that what lifts the emotions above the level of mere biological adaptation is a certain "puissance corrosive de l'interrogation" (117), which capacity Ricoeur associates with the demands of happiness and of reason (117-8). As regards human frailty, Ricoeur has two accounts which respond to our type. Early in the chapter he remarks that:

> ... la station dans le plaisir menace de figer sur place la dynamique de l'activité et de masquer l'horizon du bonheur. (110)

Later, in the course of a discussion of the person's desire to be recognized by others, he sketches another account:

> ... la fragilité de cette existence en tant que re-connue c'est que 'l'estime' qui la consacre soit seulement 'opinion, ' ... Cette nature opinante de l'estime maintient la recherche de la reconnais-sance dans la zone médiane de l'affectivité, au-des-sus du vouloir-vivre, ... mais en deçà de la sphère de l'Eros, ... (137)

This "sphère de l'Eros" is the realm of reason proper (108). The recognition of the role of culture makes this passage a more subtle account, but it remains like the former and true to our type in that it too explains human frailty by reference to some lower element, in this case "opinion, " which has somehow crept into the human make-up. Finally, as regards self-consciousness, there is an important passage which oc-curs in the same context as the passage just quoted. The quest for recognition is the highest aspiration of the human heart or "thumos" (127f.); and of it Ricoeur writes:

> Cette requête de réciprocité, dont nul vouloir-vivre

ne peut rendre compte, est le vrai passage de la
conscience à la conscience de soi. (137)

Thus, consistently with the rationalist theme, authentic self-
awareness is located at the higher pole, the goal of the transition.

It is interesting that the aspect of our type which is
least in evidence in Ricoeur is the one negative point, the
understanding of the finite and specifically of pleasure as
somehow a lower activity. There are passages which can
be interpreted in this vein, but Ricoeur is scrupulous and
often explicit (109-10, 117, 127-28) about not giving this notion the license which he does occasionally accord our other
propositions. This discrepancy in Ricoeur's treatment of
the elements of the rationalist model can perhaps be explained by the fact that the positive theses do not flatly contradict other notions--or other frameworks--which Ricoeur
also happens to value; they simply enter into an uncertain
relationship with the notions and "enrich" the exposition.
But any explicit denigration of the finite would entail a head-
on collision with other important declarations (109-10, 117,
127-28, 23-24).

Nevertheless, when all reservations have been made
there still is no escaping the fact that an understanding of
the finite as in some sense lower not only fits with the other
elements of the model which are present in Ricoeur, but is
logically required by them. I wish to indicate one or two
points at which this logical pressure makes itself felt in certain ambiguities of sense, if not finally in an ambiguity of
structure. What is crucial for this exposition is that pleasure (109), "le désir sensible" (108) and "la vie organique
qui s'achève dans la perfection instantanée du plaisir ... "
(148) have all been ranged on the side of the finite. A denigration of one is a denigration of all. Now there is a striking
passage in mid-chapter in which Ricoeur, long after he has
introduced the mediating term "coeur" and largely replaced
it with "thumos" (98), abruptly reintroduces the word and announces:

> Le 'coeur' est à la fois l'organe et le symbole de
> ce que nous venons d'appeler les 'schèmes' du
> sentiment ontologique; ... toujours le Coeur ... ap-
> paraît comme l'autre pôle du Souci; sa disponibilité
> foncière s'y oppose toujours à l'avarice du corps et
> de la vie ... (120)

On the previous page Ricoeur has said that the emotions associated with the "shemas" "constituent le pôle d'infinitude de
toute notre vie affective" (119).   Thus it would seem that for
the moment the "mediating" term has gone over altogether to
the pole of infinitude.   And appropriately enough, it is at this
same moment that the biological life-processes appear in the
most negative light, as impediments to a higher effort.

In addition, there is a passage already quoted which
holds that the simple will-to-live has no part in the attaining
of self-consciousness (137).   The astonishing thing about this
latter case is that it does not simply say, as might first appear, that the "finite" processes are lower in the eyes of
another faculty, namely reason.   Let us quote the passage
again:

> Cette requête de réciprocité, dont nul vouloir-vivre
> ne peut rendre compte, est le vrai passage de la
> conscience à la conscience de soi.   (137)

One must remember that Ricoeur has repeatedly said that
self-consciousness is the special prerogative of the emotions,
and almost their defining characteristic.   Seen in this light
the passage can hardly be read as anything but an effort to
deprive pleasure of its very birthright by saying that it is
not properly an emotion!   The suspicion is overwhelming that
in this violation we confront the true fruit of the rationalist
tendency.   In order to avoid the most glaring conflict with
Ricoeur's other statements, that tendency had somehow to
get "emotion" and "self-consciousness" together.   But within
its own premises the tendency found the greatest resistance
to that juxtaposition.   To bring the marriage off, the tendency
needed to redefine the emotions in its own terms.   Indeed it
needed to remake the emotions after its own image.

b.   the intellect/emotion framework in operation

The opening lines of the chapter on the emotions raise
the crucial question.   It is a reiteration of the question which
first made us uneasy with the conventional reading of L'homme
faillible: How is one to account for that which is specific to
the emotions?[49]   Ricoeur asks: What is there in the emotions
which has not already been observed in the intellect or in the
will (97)?

The answer which the first section of the chapter

furnishes to this question is indicated in the section's very
title, "Intentionnalité et intimité du sentiment" (99, emphasis
mine). This "inwardness" which distinguishes the emotional
life is closely comparable to the sense of belonging which we
suggested might lie at the root of self-consciousness. [50] The
link with self-consciousness was already apparent in the wording of Ricoeur's opening question, which ran, "qu'y a-t-il de
plus dans le sentiment du moi que dans le projet de l'objet
...? [51] But what is determinative is the function Ricoeur ascribes to the emotions:

> La fonction universelle du sentiment est de relier;
> ... tandis que tout le mouvement d'objectivation
> tend à m'opposer un monde, il unit l'intentionnalité
> qui me jette hors de moi à l'affection par quoi je
> me sens exister ... (147)

Ricoeur's strongest statement on the function of the emotions
is that "le sentiment engendre véritablement l'intention du
connaître à tous ses niveaux" (99, emphasis Ricoeur's). This
is bound to be somewhat puzzling. How can intentionality be
"engendered" from something other than itself? Intentionality
after all is its own sort of thing and not reducible to some
other factor. [52] But while it is not reducible, it remains
true that intentionality is a human activity and it may be that
it too is not accomplished without motivation. Ricoeur's
point, I believe, is simply that I would not attend to an object
as given were it not for some sense, however attenuated, that
"this concerns me," or that "I am involved in this." In this
connection Ricoeur speaks of "notre complicité, notre inhér-
ence, notre appartenance" (101, emphasis mine) and it is in
this sense that we spoke earlier of a sense of belonging.

Ricoeur's first section does more than make a proposal about
what distinguishes the emotions, however; it also raises a
procedural problem. In part the problem lies with ourselves
as investigators, "parce que nous vivons dans la dualité du
sujet et de l'objet qui a éduqué notre langage ... " (101).
Worse, we tend to objectify; we not only insist on the separation, but also favor one of the members. We will wish to resist this bias if we are to trace aright the workings of the
vertical framework; and there are points where we may find
Ricoeur himself at grips with the same temptation. But there
is another part of the procedural problem which resides in the
very nature of our topic; and this, I take it, is the point of
the "paradox of the emotions":

> L'aspect affectif du sentiment s'évanouit dès que
> s'efface son aspect intentionnel; ou du moins il
> s'enfonce dans une indicible obscurité ... [53]

Without constant reference to an intentionality which is not
the distinctive element in the emotions, one loses that inwardness which is distinctive.

I think that it may be possible to go a good deal further now, if we lean heavily upon the affirmation that this
aspect of the problem is rooted in the nature of the emotions
themselves and if we recall from an earlier discussion that
the paradox of the emotions is a hard paradox. [54] We may
say, first, that it is not happenstance that intentionality and
inwardness are so closely bound, but that inwardness requires intentionality for its own development and unfolding.
We may suppose, further, that it is not simply some gener-
alized intentionality which the emotions require in order to
realize their own distinctive character, but the pure case of
intentionality: the intellect. This would explain why it is
that a framework which addresses the question of what is
specific to the emotions must be a vertical framework, comprising the sphere of the emotions but also the sphere of the
intellect as well; in effect, it is because of the paradox of
the emotions that we have not simply two distinct frameworks,
but frameworks running along two wholly different axes. But
a more important effect of the proposal is to say, what Ricoeur himself never says explicitly, that at bottom the paradox of the emotions is the same as the "genèse réciproque"
of the intellect and the emotions. [55] And this makes possible
yet a further identification, our final proposal: that it is the
mediating of those poles--the intellect and (the distinctive
element within) the emotions--which will constitute the human
heart or "thumos" as it is understood within the vertical
framework.

This vertical interpretation of "thumos" differs from
the earlier, rationalist interpretation not only in the particular elements which it happens to choose as its poles, but
also in the very nature of the relationship which it entails.
The "mediation" will not be a simple transition toward one
element and away from the other, but an interaction which
heightens the specific character of each element and yet holds
the two in some ongoing interrelation. To quote again the
locus classicus for the "genèse réciproque":

> ... d'un côté le pouvoir de connaître, en se

hiérarchisant, engendre véritablement les degrés
du sentiment et arrache ce dernier à son essen-
tielle confusion; de l'autre le sentiment engendre
véritablement l'intention du connaître à tous ses
niveaux. (99)

Further, the source of the heart's restlessness will not be
the demands of one "higher" pole; it will rather be this ab-
rasive and stimulating effect which each pole has upon the
other. Similarly, the root of human frailty will not be the
backwardness of some "lower" pole, but rather the sheer
tension and instability which evolves as each pole becomes
more and more developed. Finally there is the matter of
"self-consciousness." One imagines that it will remain
where Ricoeur has explicitly set it, on the side of the emotions, and that it will develop as the emotions develop, but
that it will not be especially tied to any particular type of
emotion, such as "happiness" or "pleasure." From these
reflections we gain an alternative type to set over against
the rationalist model.

Pure types are like the gods in that they appear seldom to humankind, but their progeny are all about us. Ricoeur never does state that the "thumos" might be the mediation of intellect and emotions; and accordingly Ricoeur's
descriptions are put in terms of "finite" and "infinite," or
"pleasure" and "happiness," even when the alternative, vertical model is tacitly being used. But there is one consistent
clue which indicates when a vertical perspective is in effect.
And appropriately enough, the clue is consistent with the
motive which led us to postulate a vertical framework in the
first place and is the contrary of the denigration of pleasure
which the horizontal perspective needed to hide. 56 It is
simply that the emotions, and pleasure in particular, can be
given a positive significance in their own right--rather than
having first to be violently reinterpreted so that then, as a
consequence of the reinterpretation, the emotions, or at
least happiness, may attain a positive significance.

That this positive valuation of the emotions is deeply
rooted in the other aspects of the vertical model becomes
evident as we inspect Ricoeur's text. Let us take the model's
characteristics one by one. First, as regards the concept of
"thumos" itself, the crucial passage is that in which Ricoeur
corrects the earlier statement that "thumos" is situated "between" pleasure and happiness: "... le 'thumos' n'est pas
seulement 'situé entre' le vital et le spirituel; il est à leur

égard le 'mixte'" (144, emphasis mine; cf. 108). Clearly
the image of an amalgam is less suggestive of a transition
and more suggestive of some permanent tertium quid. And
indeed in another passage Ricoeur gives this something a
name:

> Il est remarquable que c'est dans cette région
> intermédiaire que se constitue un soi, différent
> des êtres naturels et différent d'autrui. ... c'est
> seulement avec le 'thumos' que le désir revêt le
> caractère de différence et de subjectivité qui en
> fait un Soi; ... Le Soi est en ce sens lui-même
> un 'entre-deux,' une transition (123, emphasis
> Ricoeur's).

Despite the reappearance of the term "transition," it is apparent from this passage that the self does not derive its
value solely from one "higher" pole. We shall return to this
point.

The second of the vertical model's characteristics
bears upon the question of the cause of human restlessness.
On the rationalist or finite/infinite model, the answer lay
with the demands of the infinite pole (e. g. 117). There are
passages however in which Ricoeur gives another response
in explicit contrast. In the course of a discussion of human
restlessness Ricoeur writes:

> Entre la finitude du plaisir, qui clôt un acte bien
> délimité et le scelle de son repos, et l'infini du
> bonheur, le 'thumos' glisse un indéfini et, avec
> lui, la menace qui s'attache à une poursuite sans
> fin. (142, emphasis mine).

What is the nature of this pursuit of "an indefinite," which
Ricoeur so clearly distinguishes from the pursuit of the infinite? The answer comes a few pages further on, as Ricoeur describes the way an impassioned "heart" may suddenly
fasten upon one specific object:

> ... un de ces objets soudain figure, dans une sorte
> d'immédiateté affective, le tout du désirable; on
> dirait que l'infini du bonheur descend dans l'indéfini
> de l'inquiétude; le désir du désir, âme du 'thumos,'
> offre ses objets de référence comme image, comme
> figuration ostensive, à la visée sans objet du bon-
> heur. 57

The passage concludes with a response to the third of the standard topics around which we have constructed our models, the matter of the source of human frailty. "Là est la source, là est l'occasion de toute méprise, de toute illusion." (146). But note that what is "there," "là," is not simply the opacity of the finite; it is at least as much the need, on the side of a vacuous infinite, for this representation or "figuration" in the concrete. Throughout the chapter there have been affirmations of the positive role played by the finite pole (e. g. 111-2), but in almost every case that role has been a matter of meeting the needs of actual human nature: people need incentives, people need a reward, etc. The present passage on "figuration" is one of the very few which explicitly state that the finite pole responds to needs which arise from within the infinite pole itself (cf. 115); and it is the question of the existence of that sort of need which furnishes perhaps the acid test of whether pleasure has been accorded a positive significance, or whether instead certain rationalist conceptions remain in play.

So we have come around full circle to our initial clue. One may suspect that in the process we have touched upon our fourth and final topic as well. For what are we to say of this "sorte d'immédiateté affective" which the finite pole brings to the task of "figuration"? Can the immediacy of which Ricoeur speaks be anything other than that consciousness of being involved which we have called the sense of belonging?

"La fonction universelle du sentiment est de relier ... " (147) and that function is most apparent within the vertical framework, which grounds intentionality by reaffirming in its sense of belonging the relatedness of subject and object. But "nous vivons dans la dualité du sujet et de l'objet qui a éduqué notre langage ... " (101) and thus we who reflect upon these matters gravitate spontaneously toward the horizontal framework which emphasizes not the relatedness of subject and object, but the distinction. So it is that in order to spot and appreciate the workings of the vertical framework we have been particularly in need of clues and guidelines. One which we have used from the very beginning is to watch for passages which go beyond a typology of intentions and deal with the nature and basis of intentionality as such. Another is to note the passages which treat the distinctive character of the emotions, and particularly of pleasure, in a positive manner; or alternatively to note the passages which say something positive about finitude as such. Finally and in a less abstract vein, one may simply watch for references to the sense of belonging.

Together these indicators highlight a theme which runs throughout the chapter on the emotions. At first it alternates with the finite/infinite perspective: it is the express topic of the first section (99-107) and it virtually disappears for some ten pages thereafter (109-118), with the exception of a single paragraph.[58] Then, at a point we have already noted at the foot of page 118, the vertical framework is reintroduced in a context which is genuinely supportive--significantly, a description of the "genèse réciproque"--and thereafter there is a perpetual give-and-take between the two perspectives. One of the points of contention between the two perspectives is the use to which the very notion of "belonging" should be put. Ricoeur begins by explicitly confessing that his preceding (horizontal) discussion has been in danger of overlooking "l'essentiel de la révélation du sentiment" (119). This essence, he says, resides in "l'appartenance même de l'existence à l'être" (119). The emphasis in this statement falls, I think, upon the notion of "appartenance."[59] But then shortly Ricoeur writes:

> Ce sentiment fondamental ... se spécifie dans une diversité de sentiments d'appartenance qui en sont en quelque sorte la schématisation; ces sentiments ... constituent le pôle d'infinitude de toute notre vie affective.[60]

Here in a single sentence Ricoeur brings off a total change of conceptual framework, with hardly more than the shift from "ce sentiment" to "ces sentiments" to mark the transition. In effect attention has once again been shifted away from the basis of intentionality and toward the objects of specific types of intention. In the pages which follow it takes increasing effort to make out behind the beguiling variety of objects the original underlying sense of "appartenance."

A further point of contention, which follows upon this discussion in Ricoeur, involves the entire concept of "thumos" (122ff.). But by now our "explication de texte" may have accomplished its end. Enough has been said to show that both frameworks are indeed present and voting in the chapter on the emotions; and the examination has fleshed out our understanding of the frameworks by showing how they actually function. In particular we have noted the association of the horizontal framework with a certain rationalist tendency; and

we have noted the close link between the vertical framework
and the "genèse réciproque." Having established that two
distinct frameworks are present and having examined how
they are present, we are now prepared to press one further
question. Why?

CONCLUSION:
The heart of fallibility

In the briefest terms our argument has been that in
L'homme faillible Ricoeur is doing something more than a
mere typology. The conventional or finite/infinite or horizontal interpretation has stood as a negative reference point
(negative in that it presents a quite partial truth) precisely
because that approach does look upon L'homme faillible as a
typology, developing the categories of finite intuition and infinite intention. We tried to establish and then to delimit
the partial truth of this approach under the heading of "Concepts relating to types of intention."

It is ironic, then, to discover that this effort to recognize in Ricoeur something more than a typology might itself be summarized as ... a typological study. On this
reading of it, our study shows that one can distinguish two
sets of concepts, that distinct frameworks may be erected
out of these concepts, that the frameworks in turn may under-
gird distinct models for understanding the human "heart" and
that these models are present, as types, in one chapter of
L'homme faillible. [61]

This reading of our work, like the typological reading
of Ricoeur, is true as far as it goes. But typologies have a
vested interest in distinctions and thus they tell one little,
except in merely arithmetical fashion, about underlying relationships. In the case of our frameworks the relationship is
particularly odd and thus particularly bewildering to a typological view. In effect, the horizontal framework is contained within the vertical. We can now understand in retrospect the bewilderment which we ourselves felt when, having
immersed ourselves in the horizontal view, we first ran up
against this phenomenon of collapsing. [62] What dawned upon
us then was that since the emotions give us access to the
concrete, it follows that on Ricoeur's own terms the studies
of the intellect and of the will must in some sense be tele-

77

scoped into the study on the emotions; and in large part it
was because this oddity so perplexed us that we began to
speculate on the possibility of a vertical view.

We may now be in a position to deal with that anomaly
and to summarize some of our speculation in the process.
Let us begin with a few distinctions which may prevent a re-
lapse into the earlier bewilderment. There is one quite
simple sense in which the emotions may give access to the
concrete: they may give us a feeling that we and our world
are somehow of a piece. Ricoeur seems fairly frequently
to speak of the emotions in this way (e. g. 101). I take it
that this sense is quite close to the sense of belonging which
I have suggested may lie at the root of self-consciousness. [63]
If this is so, we have here a resolution of our dilemma between the two types of response in Ricoeur to the problem of
grounding intentionality. [64] Secondly, one might conceivably
claim that beyond providing one with a certain sense, the
emotions somehow legitimate particular metaphysical statements about the concrete. I have argued that, occasional
appearances notwithstanding, Ricoeur advances such a proposal only in an attenuated form; he holds that the emotions
may give us certain clues to the nature of the metaphysically
concrete. [65] To draw conclusions from those clues various
warrants would be required, and such warrants are neither
proffered nor sought in the course of L'homme faillible.
Thirdly, one may choose to speak not of the metaphysical
but of the descriptively concrete. One might suggest that the
emotions "give access" to the descriptively concrete in the
sense that, within the particular sequence of Ricoeur's book,
the emotions furnish the final element which has been needed
in order to complete a descriptive account of what appears
to be most basic to human nature or human experience. I
think that this rather modest usage, like the first and unlike
the second, is true to L'homme faillible. After all, the
book began by studying the intellect in abstraction; only after
the emotions had been introduced could Ricoeur describe the
interaction of intellect and emotion. This interaction is of
course the "genèse réciproque" which, Ricoeur tells us, gen-
erates and develops intellect and emotion alike. [66] And it
would seem to be only common sense to suggest, as we have
done, that it is this interaction, rather than the isolated activity of the emotions per se, which constitutes in L'homme
faillible the descriptively concrete. [67]

It follows that in some respect the "genèse réciproque"
itself must constitute the framework which is most basic to

L'homme faillible; and it also follows that, again in some
respect, this common sense observation must be the sub-
stance of our own Conclusion. For we have concluded that
in L'homme faillible the metaphysically concrete has been
bracketed, which would seem to leave the field to the descriptively concrete. And the levels in terms of which we
have treated the work, namely intellect and emotion, are
comprised within the "genèse réciproque," which would seem
clearly to imply that the "genèse réciproque" is the descriptively concrete.

   But if that is the final word, why doesn't Ricoeur himself speak the word more clearly? Why doesn't he give the
"genèse réciproque" a greater emphasis? Why, to lapse for
a moment into indignant autobiography, does it require a
second or third reading before one even begins to realize
that the elusive phrase actually is a technical term?[68]   The
paradoxical answer is, I think, that while the "genèse réciproque" is indeed basic to L'homme faillible and to Ricoeur's
conception of the human, the "genèse" still does not provide
us with a single framework which we can use to interpret
that work or that conception!

   To show how this is so, I shall need to make one further distinction. Let us distinguish on the one hand the abstract and empty conception of a limit-idea, which is to say
the positing of that idea, [69] and on the other hand the actual
deployment of the idea in some instance which seeks to exemplify or pursue it. I would like to apply this distinction
to the limit-ideas which we posited some time ago[70] and to
suggest that each of these ideas may require for its deployment a specific conceptual framework which happens to have
little place for the other limit-idea. In this fashion it becomes possible to account for our paradoxical difficulty. For
when the "genèse réciproque" is conceived as consisting of
the abstract ideas, one has no framework but only bare elements; (indeed in this case we would have to say of the
"genèse réciproque" as we have said of the limit-ideas that
one cannot strictly conceive it, one can only posit it, however
validly). And when, to choose the other fork of the dilemma,
the "genèse réciproque" is rather conceived as consisting of
the two ideas in their actual deployment, one suddenly meets
with not one framework but two, set in an uneasy and ambiguous relationship. In sum, of two possible ways of looking
at the "genèse réciproque," both of them legitimate, one gives
a plurality of frameworks, the other gives none at all, and
neither permits a single, cohesive viewing of L'homme faillible.

Like the "genèse réciproque," the frameworks too may
be considered abstractly or concretely, and this distinction
may refine the statement of a moment ago that each framework allows little place for the other. In the abstract, the
frameworks are simply a pair of quite formal relationships;
and at this level it is a moot question to what extent either
can accommodate the other. It is therefore rather striking
to observe that when the frameworks act concretely as chan-
nels for the deployment of the limit-ideas, the uncertainty is
dispelled: each framework then allows the other no positive
place at all, but each reserves for the other an important,
an indispensable, negative role. The reason for this oddly
polarized situation is of course that in their deployment the
limit-ideas continue to be opposites and each continues to
require the other as a foil; as a foil only, but as a foil necessarily. Thus it is only when the vertical framework is
being used to deploy the idea of belonging that the realm of
intentionality, of subject and object, comes to be viewed
within the framework as a realm of division and alienation.
In the horizontal framework something similar occurs. The
idea of objectivity or neutrality, which can be deployed within that framework, is closely akin to the concept of "reason,"
the demand for a boundless comprehensiveness with no point
or center of reference, which Ricoeur takes from Kant.[71]
There is nothing in the horizontal framework itself which
requires that the "infinite" pole be given priority. But once
the framework has been appropriated to deploy an idea, it
naturally becomes weighted toward the pole which most near-
ly depicts that idea; and conversely the opposite pole comes
increasingly to be seen in sheerly negative terms. This may
explain the phenomenon which it took our explication de texte
to uncover: that a rationalist tendency should be so closely
associated with the horizontal framework as that framework
operates in Ricoeur's text, and yet not have any inherent
logical connection with the nature of that framework as such.

With these reflections in hand we may make our final
attack upon the question of what is most basic to L'homme
faillible. The deployment of the limit-ideas is not a simple
act but an extended process which involves an interaction--a
mutual abrasion and stimulation--between the two developing
frameworks. The quasi-hegelian character of this process
was implicit in our reflections of a moment ago. Each idea
progressively defines itself by contrast with its opposite; and
at the same time each exercises toward the other a certain
conceptual imperialism: that is, each attempts to appropriate
the opposite framework, and most crucially the opposite idea,

within its own framework. Thus the horizontal framework
attempted to interpret the emotions by ranging the possible
objects of desire along a spectrum of "les degrés du sentiment" (99) which was defined by the poles of finitude and infinitude. I think that in the last analysis it is this process
of mutual abrasion and stimulation--rather than either the abstract ideas or the concrete deployment statically conceived--
which most adequately defines the "genèse réciproque." It
is this sort of process which Ricoeur himself may have in
mind when he writes, for instance:

> Replacés dans le mouvement de leur mutuelle pro-
> motion, sentir et connaître "s'expliquent" l'un par
> l'autre ... (99)

Now if the "genèse réciproque" represents what is most basic
in L'homme faillible and if the process which we have just
described represents the fundamental sense of the "genèse
réciproque," it follows that the uneasy relationship between
these evolving frameworks will constitute the fundamental
tension at the heart of fallible man.

The task of mediating that tension will be the defining
role of the human heart or "thumos." We have seen that
each framework has its own model for understanding the
"thumos" and no doubt each is in some part true. But we
also saw that in each case certain features betrayed the fact
that the models were also a further extension of the conceptual imperialism which we noted a moment ago. In effect,
each limit-idea was trying to commandeer the very notion of
mediation. In this effort we may find the root of Ricoeur's
structural ambiguity. For if it could be made to seem that
the idea of "reason," for example, was not simply one idea
deployed within one conceptual framework, but was rather
the goal to be sought in the mediating of all frameworks,
then "reason" would have free rein over the entirety of human
nature. Thus it is true, as our textual study seemed to indicate, that the concept of "thumos" is itself the final battle-
ground. In that three-cornered contest, the authentic "thumos"
will be precisely the effort to stave off the drive from either
side toward a conceptual imperialism. It will be the effort
to mediate not simply between the finite and the infinite, nor
simply between the intellect and the emotions--but between
the limit-ideas of belonging and objectivity, each of which has
at its command a framework which makes a fair show of encompassing all of those polarities, each in its specific way.
And finally the authentic "thumos" will be the effort, by

means of this mediation, to give some coherence to human
affairs while yet recognizing that no comprehensive framework, no point of final rest, is ever to be achieved.

That I take to be the heart of fallibility.

PART 2

THE LOGIC OF THE UNCONSCIOUS
IN THE "LECTURE DE FREUD"

all he did was to remember
like the old and be honest like children.

He wasn't clever at all: he merely told
the unhappy Present to recite the Past
like a poetry lesson till sooner
or later it faltered at the line where

long ago the accusations had begun,
and suddenly knew by whom it had been judged,
how rich life had been and how silly,
and was life-forgiven and more humble,

INTRODUCTION

Hermeneutics, as it appears in Ricoeur, is never simply interpretation. It is rather a relating of interpretations. But one may relate interpretations of experience which are embodied in texts, by reflecting on ways of approaching experience, as in La symbolique du mal;[1] or one may relate interpretations of texts, by reflecting on ways of approaching texts, as in De l'interprétation and Le conflit des interprétations. In the latter case we may speak of "second-level" hermeneutics.[2]

Ricoeur's accession to the second level was prompted by a sharpened awareness of the degree to which an interpreter may have shaped a text to his or her own image; and that awareness in turn was occasioned by a confrontation with rival interpretations.[3] Thus De l'interprétation bears the subtitle Essai sur Freud. When La symbolique du mal is set beside the writings of Freud, it becomes evident that Ricoeur's hermeneutic assumed its texts to be the relatively direct expressions of relatively conscious experience. It was this two-fold assumption which licensed a method itself so direct and trusting as to be in one sense no interpretation at all, but a diligent attempt to let the phenomena exhibit themselves. Freud's approach to the same religious texts is one so distant and distrustful as to epitomize a contrasting type, which Ricoeur calls a (first-level) hermeneutic of "suspicion" (40ff.). To draw on categories which are broad but illuminating, given the history of hermeneutics,[4] Freud's suspicion is that what is manifestly proper to the domain of Culture may yet prove to be the latent outcropping of disguised Nature, indirect in its manner and unconscious in its origins.

In the one instance a direct approach is the correlate of an assumption that the texts are straightforwardly expressive, in the other an indirect approach arises from the suspicion of deceit. But this is not reason enough to award Freud the title of greater sophistication. The dispute between

the freudians and their opponents has by long tradition been
over the very question of whose subtlety is warranted, and
whose spurious. Now the short way with freudians is to
turn their device upon themselves: to ask, for example,
why they are so attached to this father figure, Freud. But
such a tactic is sheerly critical; indeed it falls little short
of achieving a philosophic translation of the demand of an
eye for an eye. Ricoeur prefers a longer path, but one
which may eventuate in rapprochement; he extends to Freud
the courtesy of the interpretive approach which he, Ricoeur,
has been defending. [5] Thus the question of where the authentic complexity may lie is discreetly tabled until the concluding "Dialectique" (331ff.). The body of De l'interprétation--
the "Analytique" or "Lecture de Freud" (65-330)--is a patient
pursuit of the manifest sense of Freud's own texts, an inquiry not into the justification so much as into the nature of
the complexity which Freud propounds.

a. against the charge of reductionism

       Ricoeur's eventual conclusion is that the latent Nature
which Freud hypothesizes always retains certain logical connections with, and thus certain logical dependencies upon, the
manifest Culture which served as his starting point. In Ricoeur's terms, Freud's "langage de force" is never independent of a "langage de sens," his "énergétique" is always also
a "herméneutique." Indeed Ricoeur asserts, in a dictum to
which we shall recur throughout our discussion of Freud:
"ce discours mixte est la raison d'être de la psychanalyse."
(75, emphasis mine) Thus the conclusion that in principle
and in execution Freud is never totally the reductionist.

       Ricoeur proposes to demonstrate this by singling out
those freudian terms which do seem to portray mental processes as sheerly mechanical, and pursuing their logic to its
end. The pursuit repeats and plays upon a cycle which may
be sketched in five recurrent steps. To spell out this model
argument is illuminating because Ricoeur's singleness of
theme--the "discours mixte"--at the same time that it lends
his study an impressive unity, does little to alert the reader
to the various phases of argument. The "langage de force"/
"langage de sens" distinction shifts functions unannounced;
and the reader may be left with a general sense of where
Ricoeur is headed but no certainty of where he is. [6]

       1. Report. Ricoeur's point of departure is invariably

some writing of Freud's; he makes it clear that he himself
does not speak from a firsthand knowledge of analysis (xi).
At this stage the phrase "langage de force" functions rather
literally, denoting particularly those words, such as "psychic
energy" and "repression," which Freud adopted from the
physics of his day.

2. Text. From the report Ricoeur isolates the evidence which, in the particular case, served as Freud's
touchstone. In an empirical science this evidence would be
the "data"; but, in keeping with his argument, Ricoeur insists that the logic of psychoanalysis has its starting point
not in facts of Nature but in stretches of language, i. e.
written or spoken "texts" such as an instance of free association or the recounting of a dream, which clearly pertain
to the sphere of Culture. Since "Nature" and "Culture" on
the one hand and "langage de force" and "langage de sens"
on the other are roughly parallel expressions of Ricoeur's
guiding theme, it follows that there is a sense in which it
is tautologically true that the text consists entirely of "langage de sens. " And yet what is of interest in the text, what
constitutes the evidence strictly speaking, is precisely the
point at which the normal fabric of sense yields to a rent or
a snarl: something has been forgotten, something seems al-
lusive or incoherent.

3. Text & construct. Ricoeur then checks Freud's
theoretical constructs against the evidence which engendered
them. During this phase of the argument Ricoeur's "languages" seem to function as relational terms. "Langage de
sens" denotes those constructs or aspects of constructs
which bear rather directly, hardly more than descriptively,
upon the text at hand. And "langage de force" now refers
to that whereby the constructs outrun the evidence in the
direction of speculative hypothesis--or gratuitous speculation.

4. Construct & construct. It tends to fall out that
the terms which are on loan from physics and the terms
which exceed the apparent evidence are one and the same.
These alien terms, on two counts "langage de force, " Ricoeur proceeds to examine in their own right, in their various conceptual relations. His observation is that this "langage économique" is invariably set in close relation to terms
of another sort. These partner-terms are such that they do
not simply exemplify the experience of meaning, as did the
"langage de sens" of the second phase and as does any langage short of gibberish: they refer to that experience, and

it is in this respect that they are called "langage intentionnel. " Examples would be the concepts "idea, " "fantasy, "
"representation. " It is in this phase of study, Ricoeur be-
lieves, that the crucial issue is posed:

> L'essentiel, pour une critique philosophique, con-
> cerne ce que j'appelle le lieu de ce discours éner-
> gétique. Son lieu, me semble-t-il, est à la flexion
> du désir et du langage; c'est de ce lieu que nous
> essayerons de rendre compte par l'idée d'une ar-
> chéologie du sujet. C'est bien à la soudure du
> "naturel" et du "signifiant" que la poussée de la
> pulsion est "représentée" par l'affect et l'idée;
> c'est pourquoi la coordination du langage écono-
> mique et du langage intentionnel est la grande
> question de cette épistémologie et ne peut être
> éludée par réduction à l'un ou à l'autre.[7]

5. Construct & report. The "langage de force"
looked passing strange when it was first tested against the
text in step 3, but now the matter may be addressed less
brusquely and rather by way of analogy. We may ask: is
there not in the text some "x" such that "x" is to the manifest "langage de sens" as the "langage économique" is to the
"langage intentionnel" of step 4? This approach may differ
only relatively from the earlier critique in step 3, but it has
the merit of permitting the "langage de force" to gather its
full context of meaning, its web of conceptual relations, before it is pressed for its referent. This forbearance is re-
warded in that hitherto unnoticed aspects of the text begin to
emerge, and recognized facets take on a new significance.
There is a moment of analytic insight.

That insight may provide the occasion for another
cycle of interpretation. More importantly for our present
concerns, it serves Ricoeur as a partial validation of Freud's
peculiar hermeneutic. Not that the "langage de force" ever
yields total transparency and not that Freud's account has
been transmuted into scientific explanation; but rather that a
terminology which had seemed an uncritical mimicking of a
fashionable physics or a studied adoption of that physics with
reductionist intent has rather proved itself, in the moment of
insight, a viable tool for the understanding of cultural phenomena.

Having formulated Ricoeur's defense of Freud against
the charge of reductionism, we may speculate for a moment

on how this defense may bear upon our own concern, the
concept of mystery. Our introductory discussion of mystery
was set against the background of Ricoeur's earlier work;
it may help us to reintroduce the topic if we first note a few
points of comparison between the earlier writings and the
present defense of Freud. First, the fact that the payoff of
Ricoeur's defense should come, as we have said, when "hitherto unnoticed aspects of the text begin to emerge" brings to
mind the method of Le volontaire et l'involontaire. That the
argument should turn upon "a moment of analytic insight"
suggests how close Ricoeur's method still is to that of phenomenology and specifically to the "diagnostique. "[8] Once
again an alien and objective approach, in this case the application of a "langage de force" to mental processes, has been
brought around to the point that it may be partially appropriated in terms of that which presents itself to consciousness,
i. e. in terms of insights formulable by a "langage de sens. "
There is the difference, however, that in De l'interprétation,
more clearly than in Le volontaire et l'involontaire, Ricoeur
recognizes the partiality of the appropriation. Indeed he at-
tributes positive significance to the fact that the "langage de
force" resists a total appropriation.

          This last remark is sure to trigger a further associ-
ation. There is a striking parallel between the "langage de
force"/"langage de sense" relationship and the relationship
among the various modes of discourse which make up the
"symbolique. "[9] With this comparison we do indeed catch a
glimpse of one side of our fundamental argument regarding
mystery. We resolved early on that the goal of winning
from Freud a certain concept of mystery was to be reached
by going through Freud rather than around him. It would be
cold comfort if the guardians of culture, and among them the
practitioners of religion, were simply to congratulate themselves on having disclosed that Freud is not a simpleminded
reductionist. For it remains that while Freud may not have
reduced cultural phenomena to forces operating entirely outside or beneath the cultural realm, he did submit that realm
as one conventionally assumes it to a most thorough-going
critique. The possibility of authentic religious practice has
not been arbitrarily disallowed, but it has been brought seriously into question by a critique which is rendered the more
telling by its very sophistication. Our argument must take
this into account. It shall therefore propose that the psychoanalytic critique which does indeed call into question a particular case of mystery, such as the mystery of evil as at-
tested by religious confession, is accomplished by means of

constructs which tacitly affirm another case of that concept, namely the mystery of the body.

The key to the argument is the retention within Freud's constructs of two distinct and irreducible ways of talking about incarnate experience, the "langage de sens" and the "langage de force," corresponding roughly to Marcel's lived-body and body-as-object. And of course the crucial point within that key is not the correspondence with Marcel, but the sheerly formal observation that some two-fold division, whatever its nature, does in fact persist. That point is already enough to demonstrate that a certain notion of mystery is at work. For each of the two languages shows by its persistence that the other is not wholly sufficient, and thus that our knowledge is no more than analogical.[10] But while it is adequate in principle, this argument remains extremely formal; and, further, it draws upon only one of our two guidelines regarding the concept of mystery. One may suspect that there will yet be occasion to recall our second guideline-- the perplexity over the relation between the disparate languages or points of view.[11]

b.   for "an archeology of the subject"

The occasion does indeed arise; and, procedurally, it is important that it comes in connection with a problem which is not of our devising but entirely intrinsic to Ricoeur's own exposition. The problem in brief is that Ricoeur's defense of Freud against the charge of reductionism may have succeeded all too well. It almost seems that Freud has been made over in the image of a genial--and finally uninteresting--common sense.

In its earliest form, Freud's "langage de force" was consciously and almost willfully literalistic, the very embodiment of what Ricoeur has called "... le caractère indépassable du désir" (70); the "langage" purported to denote actual places and forces--neurons and impulses--within the physical brain (79ff.). But Freud discarded his literalism early and expressly, along with the unsuccessful "Project for a Scientific Psychology" (79ff.); and thereafter he would seem to have looked upon the "langage de force," in its subsequent manifestations, as no more than a convenient fiction. In the New Introductory Lectures he wrote, "The theory of the instincts is so to say our mythology. " This clearly suggests that the present dissension between "langage de force" and "langage de sens" might eventually be reconciled in a single demythologized terminology.[12]   Ricoeur himself seems to propose nothing less:

> ... j'estime que le développement du freudisme
> peut être considéré comme la progressive réduc-
> tion de la notion "d'appareil psychique"--au sens
> d'une "machine qui ne tarderait pas à fonctionner
> d'elle-même"--à une topique où l'espace n'est plus
> un lieu mondain, mais une scène sur laquelle en-
> trent en débat des rôles et des masques; cet es-
> pace deviendra lieu du chiffre et du déchiffrage.[13]

The transformation would seem to be total, from a space
defined by the cranium and inhabited by physical forces to a
metaphorical "space" which is rather the realm of social
discourse. By all appearances the business of translation
or "déchiffrage" which occupies the latter, metaphorical
"space" might be conducted and described entirely in terms
of "langage de sens." There is no assurance that psychoanalysis will not soon be relieved of the mixed discourse
which Ricoeur himself has termed the discipline's "raison
d'être."

> But--Ricoeur goes on to append a qualification.

> Certes, le principe de constance maintiendra
> jusqu'au bout une certaine extériorité de l'expli-
> cation énergétique à l'égard de l'interprétation
> du sens par le sens; la "topique" gardera tou-
> jours un caractère ambigu; on pourra y voir à
> la fois le développement de la théorie primitive
> de l'appareil psychique et un long mouvement
> pour s'en affranchir. (80, emphasis mine)

Moreover the qualification, with its admission of ambiguity,
remains ambiguous itself. To clear this up, we may begin
by setting out the options. 1) The simplest view has already been suggested. It would hold that the evolution of
Freud's thought is a progressive refinement culminating in
a pure "langage de sens" which would, in consequence, become the norm for extricating the true Freud from the de-
tritus of nineteenth century physics. This is the only view
which the qualification would clearly disallow. 2) It is a
measure of the ambiguity that a mere variant of this simplest
view could be enough to accommodate the qualification. One
need only add that it happened that for extraneous reasons
the goal of pure "langage de sens" was never fully attained.
Freud never quite freed himself of his unfortunate infatuation

with a mechanistic physics.   This is more or less the view
from which a variety of freudian revisionists would draw a
mandate to amend the work of the master in order to carry
it nearer its own alleged goal. [14]   Between the first and second view the basic logic stays the same; they differ only on
the question of whether that logic was ever fully realized.
It is therefore fitting to house them under a single rubric:
we may speak of a "linear" view.

     Now we have already noted that Ricoeur has said of
Freud's thought that:

> ... la coordination du langage économique et du
> langage intentionnel est la grande question de cette
> épistémologie et ne peut être éludée par réduction
> à l'un ou à l'autre. [15]

For Ricoeur, in effect, the revisionists are merely reductionists of another sort. [16]   But how tricky it is to actually thread
one's way between the various impoverishments of Freud is
made evident by the ambiguities which we have sampled within Ricoeur's own remarks.   Witness also the quandaries be-
setting the one alternative view which would seem to remain
open to Ricoeur.   3)   One might posit a similarity between
the evolution of the freudian languages and the development
of the several modes of discourse which comprised the "symbolique. "[17]   It would then be possible to argue that some form
of the "langage de force" survives not merely as a fortuitous
vestige, but as a vocabulary charged with a significance of
its own and providing the "langage de sens" with a needed
complement or foil.   But this line of argument is only as
strong as its initial premise; and the similarity of the two
evolutions is made questionable by the fact that within the
"symbolique" the part of the mode of discourse most resistant to understanding was played by a straightforward literalism which held, for example, that the sinful man was phys-
ically unclean. [18]   It was a literalism of just this sort, a
reference to physical fact, which Freud so carefully renounced.

     Nevertheless this third option has headed us in the
right direction.   If Freud is to retain his peculiar character
and interest, the "langage de force" must somehow be retained; and that means that we must find in the concept sufficient integrity and ... force, that it can claim and defend
a function of its own.   The lesson of the third option, in its
promise and its failure, is that there must not be assigned
to the "langage de force" a single physical referent and that,

at the same time, there must be attributed to it a certain logical force. But this is as much as to say that the "langage de force" must be conceived as a principle.

Such a course would have implications for the method which we have thus far reconstructed from Ricoeur. To discern principles and debate them, one would have to incorporate into that method a further level which would be more consciously systematic in its manner. In retrospect it becomes apparent how unwaveringly descriptive were all five of the stages of Ricoeur's defense. It was no accident that the procedure could be compared to the phenomenology of Le volontaire et l'involontaire. Even the stage 4 of "construct & construct" asked only that one observe the association--in truth, hardly more than the juxtaposition--of the two vocabularies in question. Moreover we may begin to have second thoughts about the fact that the argument drew its persuasiveness from the moment of analytic insight. Isn't this rather too reminiscent of the "diagnostique"--for which the unitary viewpoint of phenomenology was finally definitive and for which all other languages and testimonies were, like Kierkegaard's Socrates or Wittgenstein's scaffolding, finally dispensable?

It is this retention of the descriptive method which lies, I think, at the heart of the present problem. The method was suited to the defense of Freud against the charge of reductionism; but left to itself it turns counterproductive. For description can discern Freud's terms only under the aspect of their surface characteristics--the lexicon they are drawn from, the referents they seem to have--and those characteristics have little to do with certain deeper, systematic implications. [19] But it is at this systematic level that Freud, with growing sophistication, increasingly located the issues which define his peculiar approach. Thus the irony that as Freud's distinctive method sinks deeper its roots, and as Ricoeur's thesis regarding the centrality of the "discours mixte" is thus increasingly confirmed, that confirmation becomes less and less apparent to the method which Ricoeur has generally assumed. In the end the widespread conviction that Freud gradually acceded to the suasions of common sense may tell more about the methods of the investigators than about their subject. The moral in short is that as long as one retains the method of the linear view, one will not find a way to anything other than linear conclusions.

I would propose therefore that we set aside the issue

of literalism, pro or con, as a misplaced argument and that
we pry loose the concept of "langage de force" from the notion of a specific vocabulary. The trick, however, will be
to do this and yet retain something like the model of the
"symbolique. " For it is only by showing that the relation
between Freud's "languages" is somehow like the relationship which obtains between the modes of discourse within
the "symbolique" that we will win for the "langage de force"
a permanent place and thus succeed in reconstructing the
middle course which Ricoeur would have us steer between
the reductionists and the revisionists. Specifically, the
trick will be to demonstrate that some sort of opacity, something reminiscent of the primitive literalism within the "symbolique, " survives Freud's own abandonment of literalism;
and to show that this opacity continues to perform an indispensable function in the subsequent stages of the freudian
system. It is commonly assumed that as Freud loses his
literalism, he loses his bite. But that needn't be. Our
task is thus to show that Freud always held, and held successfully, a "hard" notion of the unconscious.

    The difference between this task and that of the de-
fense of Freud against the charge of reductionism is that in
the present case one must show not simply that two languages exist in Freud nor even simply that there are two
principles, but that there is specifically a duality of princi-
ples--duality being understood as the retention of the two,
but also more positively as a certain interrelation between
them. [20]   The difference is a corollary of the shift from a
descriptive to a more systematic method. In locating the
crucial issue of Freud's peculiar hermeneutic at this point
of systematic interrelation, we simply confirm the importance which Ricoeur himself assigned to "la flexion du désir
et du langage" or "la soudure du 'naturel' et du 'signifiant', "
and with Ricoeur we may say, "c'est de ce lieu que nous es-
sayerons de rendre compte par l'idée d'une archéologie du
sujet. "[21] In postulating that the interrelation is a duality,
we imply that the two principles may interact, that they may
even be in need of one another, but that in some specific
sense they will be finally irreconcilable. But just what that
specific sense might be, and just what can be gained from
our "archeology, " can be gathered only inductively. Whatever be the truth of his disputed kinship to nineteenth century physics, it is at least certain that Freud's principles
are not subject without caricature to a single formulaic statement. Even less can this be true of the relationship between
them.

Enough may have been said however to suggest one
further view of Freud's evolution. 4) Let us call it a
"dialectical" view. A key text would be the conclusion of
Ricoeur's ambiguous passage of qualification:

> ... on pourra y voir à la fois le développement de
> la théorie primitive de l'appareil psychique et un
> long mouvement pour s'en affranchir. [22]

The passage would be interpreted in the sense of two principles presiding over lines of development which are concur-
rent but distinct, and even at odds. The lines would be
capable of impinging upon one another and of responding to
the impingements. But the responses would not necessarily
be in the direction of accommodation, as various revisionist
views might assume. A response could equally well be a
matter of each line's taking cognizance of the other in order
to pursue the more shrewdly the course dictated by its own
autonomous principle. In summary, then: The linear view
did conceive of the "langage de force" as developing, but only in the sense that it evolved into something other than itself. The interpretation on analogy with the "symbolique,"
in contrast, did discern in the "langage" an abiding significance; but this residuum stood or was carried along like a
stone in a stream, while the real development rolled on
around it. What the dialectical view proposes, in contrast
to both of these, is a duality which is neither surrendered
nor simply retained, but which is elaborated and amplified
in the course of its successive instances.

The dialectic of principles within the human psyche,
as that psyche was understood by Freud at any given moment,
is something different from the dialectic of those same principles as they operated within the logic of Freud's own evolution. It is, in effect, the difference between Freud's view
of the development of the self and the development of Freud's
view of the self. But the concerns are connected intimately;
and it is only when both have been lifted into view--when
Freud has been seen synchronically and diachronically, as it
were--that one can pronounce on Freud's view of the self. [23]
In anticipation of that inductive study, however, it is possible
to say that if in the end there does emerge a genuine duality
of principles, then Ricoeur's "archeology of the subject," or
our reconstruction of it, will have far outrun Ricoeur's simple
defense of Freud. For it will have been shown that while the
"langage de force" is not autonomous, there is some important respect in which the same is true, as well, of the

"langage de sens. " Again, just what that "important respect" may be can be gathered only inductively. But it may be enough to give testimony to the inexhaustibility of the concrete and thus further evidence of the actuality of a certain concept of mystery. An archeology of the subject is also an archeology of sense. [24]

THE QUESTION OF DEVELOPMENT

Our Introduction distinguished two facets of Ricoeur's study of Freud: the defense of Freud against the charge of reductionism and the project for "an archeology of the subject." And it made the distinction in two different ways: with regard to the perspective on Freud and with regard to the method from which each perspective arose. That Freud was not a reductionist can be shown by a method which is largely descriptive; but to demonstrate that Freud's thought entails a certain "archeology" requires that one reach beyond mere description to a method which is systematic as well.

Now if we glance through De l'interprétation with this four-fold discrimination in mind, an imbalance becomes apparent. For in the most systematic section, namely the concluding "Dialectique, " the two perspectives receive fairly equal attention. The major theses of the opening chapter in that section--"Que la psychanalyse n'est pas une science d'observation" and "Que la psychanalyse n'est pas la phénoménologie" (350ff. , 380ff.)--closely parallel the defense and the archeology respectively. And there is in the "Dialectique" an entire chapter given over to the archeology alone (407ff.). But throughout the more descriptive "Analytique, " and thus throughout half of the entire work, it is the defense which predominates.

This tilting of the discussion toward the concerns of the defense of Freud against the charge of reductionism is in part a reflection of the questions which first prompted Ricoeur to write on psychoanalysis; and in part it stems from the logic of his argument, since in the nature of things a relatively descriptive reading must precede a more systematic reconstruction. Yet a further explanation may be suggested by the very titles "Analytique" and "Dialectique. " Ricoeur appears to have consciously chosen to isolate the two moments of his method, presumably in order to insure that his eventual reflections will have their basis in a reading of the freudian texts which has been unprejudiced and undistracted.

From where we stand, however, as readers of Ricoeur, that descriptive reading has been accomplished; it is preserved in Ricoeur's own text. There is less reason therefore why we ourselves should persist in so strict a methodological separation. And there are good reasons why we should not. For one thing, Ricoeur is simply unable within the "Dialectique" to give an adequate demonstration of the extent to which an archeology has indeed been implied throughout the entire span of the "Analytique"; this is so partly because he hasn't the space and partly because his conceptual supply lines have been overextended. But such a demonstration is needed. For another thing, there is the cumulative impression created by all that vast stretch of description. In principle and in the end, of course, description furthers the archeology as much as it does the defense, and thus may issue in a balanced account of Freud. But sheerly in terms of the impression it creates, the long stretch of isolated description largely unattended by reflection leans heavily toward the side of the defense--and thus threatens to play into the hands of the revisionist camp. All that meets the eye is the fact that Freud's most mechanistic conceptions are revised repeatedly and absorbed; by all appearances, the master is being converted to common sense.

What we need to do, therefore, is to draw the two methods more closely together. Thus our own strategy will be to follow each step of the "Analytique" and in each instance to carry through the systematic reflection on the spot. In each case we will begin by noting the emphasis and conclusions which emerge when Ricoeur's text is regarded as simple description; we will then show how these emphases shift and become more balanced once one pauses to discern and extend the systematic implications. As our own space is limited, the demonstration will often amount to indicating that the material can be given first one outline and then, with greater justice, another.

I. THE FIRST TOPOGRAPHY:
Unconscious, preconscious & conscious

In the course of his development Freud introduced three major configurations: the first topography of unconscious, preconscious and conscious; the second topography of id, ego and superego (in French: ça, moi et surmoi); and the late, quasi-mythological dualism of Eros and Thanatos (to which Ricoeur adds a third member, Ananké or "Necessity").

The three parts of Ricoeur's "Analytique" correspond to these successive innovations; and the chapters within each part generally correspond to some writing or group of related writings which advance the particular configuration. Our own study will follow Ricoeur's outline, with minor variations. Thus each of our subsections will generally correspond to a chapter in Ricoeur and a work or group of works in Freud.

a. The "Project for a Scientific Psychology"[25]

     Freud opens his early and somewhat speculative "Project for a Scientific Psychology" with a programmatic statement which may stand as a locus classicus of the "langage de force."

> The project involves two principal ideas: 1. That what distinguishes activity from rest is to be regarded as a quantity (Q) subject to the general laws of motion. 2. That it is to be assumed that the material particles in question are the neurons. [26]

But in the course of the "Project" itself and in Freud's notes and letters during this early period it becomes evident that a certain minimum of concern for the givens of human experience is inescapable; and that even that minimal concern is enough to drive Freud's original program into incoherence (83). What happens in effect is that in the course of Freud's considerations there emerges, almost without his having willed it or wanted it, a forerunner of what he will eventually call the "ego."[27]

     In describing this development Ricoeur focusses upon the first of the two fundamental premises from Freud's programmatic statement, the quantitative hypothesis. This is appropriate, for it is upon the notion of quantity that Freud's "Project" relies for its coherence; if the concept of quantity proves unequal to this task, the effort fails not simply in one respect but in the entirety of its fabric. Now there are a number of counts on which the quantitative hypothesis does in fact fall short; in effect the existence of those psychic activities which Freud will eventually call "secondary processes" has already made itself felt (84, 85, 86-90). Thus for example perceptual activity, which enters via the crucial notion of "satisfaction." Freud's theory cannot do without some notion of satisfaction to denote the final stage of a postulated cycle, when the psychic machinery is once again at rest; but

the notion of satisfaction violates the equally indispensable
premise of the self-contained character of the psychic mechanism, because "il met en jeu le monde extérieur (nourriture,
partenaire sexuel)" (86). And if nevertheless one does assume a self-contained psychic system, further evidence of
secondary process continues to crop up, even within that
sphere. For it becomes apparent that not all energy is free-
floating; some of it is bound or "liée" (84).

It was under the cumulative pressure of factors such
as these that Freud eventually abandoned his original "Project" (92). A convenient index of this process is his gradual
surrender of the second of the premises he originally enumerated, the anatomical reference (91-2). At the same time, in
a more positive vein, one may discern in Freud's grudging
admission of certain secondary processes a premonition that
he himself may adopt an authentically hermeneutical interpretation (92-4). Granted, vestiges of a quasi-mechanistic viewpoint will never be entirely exorcized: Freud remained a
strict determinist to the end (94). But already, in this most
recalcitrant of his writings, we have the germ of a perspective which will not be covertly anatomical, but genuinely
"psychique" (92).

That much about the "Project" is undisputed, and thus
may be reckoned as simple description. The debatable point
is the development's significance. On the face of it the answer would seem to be clear. Let us be entirely explicit,
in order to ferret out the assumptions of this prima facie
account: Freud began by postulating "a machine which in a
moment would run of itself."[28] Such a machine, at once
actual and autonomous, was the logical offspring of the marriage of two hypotheses, one anatomical and the other quanti-
tative. To use Freud's later terminology, the machine represented a proposal that the human mind be understood as
consisting entirely of primary processes. But Freud was
compelled to acknowledge certain secondary processes. Ipso
facto he was forced to surrender some of the machine's autonomy. The machine was dependent upon certain external
relations; and even within the psyche there were certain impediments to the free flow of energy. Now the original machine was the forerunner of Freud's concept of the id, as
our reference to primary processes suggests. Thus one may
say, with an eye to Freud's subsequent development, that
Freud has already placed constraints upon the autonomy of
the id--and thus, by extension, upon the autonomy of the unconscious.

In this prima facie account we witness a description of Freud giving birth, by scarcely perceptible steps, to a linear interpretation. That steps have nevertheless been taken, and certain assumptions made, becomes evident if one remarks that a little knowledge is proverbially a dangerous thing and that there is no reason to suppose that a little secondary process is, per se, any better. If it is true that Freud has acknowledged in the unconscious certain secondary processes, it is equally true that the processes have been located in the unconscious; and one has in the nature of the secondary processes no guarantee of the ends which they will pursue, once they are beyond the range of conscious inspection. To ever have assumed that one did have such a guarantee is, of course, a rationalist fallacy.

The linear interpretation of Freud, like the rationalist view of itself, is not so much wrong as it is incomplete. By the same token the strength of a dialectical interpretation lies in its ability to subsume the alternative account and make good the shortcomings of that account. In effect the line of development upon which the linear account fastened so single-mindedly becomes one of two interacting lines on the dialectical view. But the second line is not a descriptive datum which just happened to have been overlooked; it is rather a set of implications which need to be brought to light. The best way to rebut the rationalist fallacy, then, is to make a second run at Ricoeur's description with an eye to its systematic implications.

At the outset Freud postulated, in a pure instance of "langage de force," "a machine which in a moment would run of itself."[29] It is the direct consequence of the advent of secondary process, which is to say, of "énergie liée,"[30] that now the machine can somewhat inhibit its immediate responses, thereby stepping back, as it were, and posing itself against its environment. As Ricoeur himself says of the concept of secondary process:

> C'est en réalité le désintéressement du savant, sa capacité d'immobilité et de repos sur l'idée, qui sont transcrits en termes énergétiques. (90)

Add perception, as Freud does--and, to extend a metaphor, nothing is wanted for the machine to have become fully cybernetic! This I take to be the import of Ricoeur's summary observation that:

> C'est un point acquis pour toujours: investissement
> constant du moi, fonction d'inhibition, épreuve de la
> réalité iront toujours ensemble. (88)

In effect, Freud's early anticipation of the ego, the "investissement constant du moi," embodies and will continue to embody a heightened autonomy which results from the capacity
for inhibition.

What has happened, in brief, is this. The descriptive
account accurately observed that Freud set out with the hypotheses a) that the mind is autonomous in the sense of a
self-contained energy system and b) that it is internally simple, its energy free-floating. In the course of his thought
Freud tacitly surrendered the first point, about the absence
of relations--but he surrendered the second as well. The
contribution of a more systematic account is simply to note
that the latter revision has an important effect upon the former. One is forced to distinguish different senses of "autonomy." Certainly the cybernetic autonomy is relative, as opposed to the absolute autonomy of the original hypothesis;
this much must be conceded to the linear interpretation. But
it is no less certain that the new-found autonomy is cybernetic, that it belongs to a higher level and that in this sense
the autonomy has been heightened.

Such is the result of a more systematic approach to
this early stage of Freud's evolution. Now if the original
conception of the machine was the forerunner of the id, the
revised conception is the forerunner of the interaction of the
ego and the id. From that interaction there has emerged a
certain higher form of autonomy; and, if the machine is still
the same machine in any sense at all, that autonomy will, in
some part, be placed at the service of the machine's original
purposes, which are also the purposes of the id. One result
of the introduction into the psyche of secondary processes will
simply be a more cunning pursuit of what Freud will eventually call "the pleasure principle." When matters are regarded
thus, in the light of purposes or principles, it becomes much
less certain that Freud is moving away from the sort of natural, machine-like autonomy which is epitomized in the "langage de force"; and it is in fact certain that to some unspecified extent that autonomy has actually been heightened--not
in spite of, but because of, the introduction of secondary
processes. That is the crucial point which is made by a
dialectical interpretation.

b. The Interpretation of Dreams[31]

Our commentary upon Freud's "Project" made the
point that in abandoning the hypothesis of an anatomical referent, in abandoning one conception of the autonomy of the
unconscious and finally in abandoning the "Project" itself,
Freud was not necessarily surrendering every conception of
the autonomy of the unconscious. With the essay on The Interpretation of Dreams Freud made a new start; whereas the
"Project" was by its nature an exercise in pure "langage de
force," the present essay bases much of its case on such
cultural phenomena as the recounting of dreams and in so
doing it accords the "langage de sens" an important place.
The heart of this development is, I believe, Freud's introduction of the concept of a certain distortion or transformation, which lays the foundation for Freud's "discours mixte"
(as Ricoeur explicitly observes, p. 99), for the "archeology
of the subject" (as I understand Ricoeur to imply) and for a
certain abiding duality (as I shall progressively argue).

Since Ricoeur does note the importance of Freud's innovation, there is no need for us to duplicate that task (99ff.).
What one does miss in Ricoeur's exposition, however, is an
adequate indication of the logic which makes necessary the
innovation. The result is that the "discours mixte," and by
extension the "archeology of the subject," do not seem logically compelling. The cause of this lacuna would seem to
be, once again, the somewhat descriptive character of Ricoeur's exposition. It follows that our own commentary
should include a quick summary of Ricoeur's exposition of
the freudian innovation, an illustration of the descriptive character of the exposition, an indication that something important is missing, a supplementary exposition and a demonstration that the supplement plugs the gap.

Ricoeur's exposition is again played against the back-
drop of the protean distinction of "langage de sens" and "langage de force." The key textual peculiarity Freud isolated
in the dream accounts which he examined is overdetermina-
tion (110-1). This textual peculiarity he then proposed to explain by the mechanisms of condensation and displacement (101).
Were matters to remain at that, Freud's talk about "mechanisms" could not be taken as anything more than so many figures of speech: dream analysis could readily disregard such
"explanations," and operate entirely within the realm of
"sense"--specifically, within the realm of certain commonly
recognized rhetorical devices (111). But Freud's meditation

upon the textual peculiarity leads him to find peculiar another
matter, which heretofore had seemed so natural as to require no explanation. This is the simple fact that dreams
consist of images at all.

> ... la 'transposition' ou 'distorsion' (Verstellung)
> qu'opère l'interprétation du contenu manifeste vers
> le contenu latent, découvre une autre transposition,
> celle même du désir en images et à laquelle Freud
> consacre le chapitre IV. (99, emphasis Ricoeur's)

In postulating this fundamental transposition of desire, conceived as an act of force, into the images which will make
up the dream text, Freud makes his most explicit and fundamental commitment to the mixed vocabulary of "langage de
force" and "langage de sens" which will be, henceforth, the
earmark of his hermeneutic. In associating with the rhetorical peculiarities of the dream text certain "explanations,"
and especially in postulating this fundamental "explanation"
of the fact that there is a text at all, psychoanalysis defines
its very nature.

But the "explanation" as such is nothing more than a
postulate: it itself needs to be explained. As Ricoeur observes, "la figuration fait problème et Freud a construit
toute une métapsychologie de la régression pour en rendre
compte."[32] The second section of Ricoeur's chapter (109f.)
deals with Freud's initiation of that metapsychology in his
own Chapter VII. Ricoeur notes three stages to Freud's argument and he distinguishes them in terms which are relatively descriptive: the first introduces concepts which are
quasi-spatial in character, the second introduces concepts
which are temporal and the third takes account of conflict.[33]
Of these stages, it is the second which deals with the drive
toward fulfillment and thus with figuration as an activity.
Freud postulates at the level of the unconscious proper a
"nostalgie du stade primitif du désir hallucinatoire," the consequence of an early and ineradicable association within the
primary process (114). This nostalgia is what is most basic
to the metapsychology--"le processus primaire est bien primaire" (117)--and it is the explanation of why there should
be figuration at all (114). In contrast, the secondary processes which are discussed in the third stage are judged to
serve the purposes of the primary process and to be derivative from it (115f.). Thus, in the words with which Ricoeur
brings his own chapter to a close:

'L'appareil' que le chapitre VII cerne en ses trois
essais successifs, c'est l'homme en tant qu'il a
été et reste Chose. (119, emphasis Ricoeur's)

Now I wish to suggest that on this account it is in no
wise certain that the fundamental "explanation" can be any
more successful than were the initial, secondary "explanations" in resisting the proposal that this whole business be
collapsed into "langage de sens. " Why shouldn't we look
upon dream interpretation as simply a type of translation,
from a manifest text to a "latent" text? (cf. 96f.) And why
shouldn't we apply Occam's razor, reading the various references to psychic mechanisms in much the same vein as we
read references to divine providence, special and general, in
the writings of early astronomers: namely as stopgap notions, provisional conventions awaiting eventual elucidation--
elucidation in the "langage de sens"?   "Condensation" and
"displacement" would simply be conventions for discovered or
undiscovered inter-linguistic relations which happen to be
more complex than a simple one-to-one (cf. 100); and the
postulate of a fundamental transposition or distortion, so far
from being embraced as psychoanalysis' act of self-definition,
would be discarded as pointless speculation. Such a proposal is entirely contrary to Ricoeur's intention, of course (99),
but that is precisely the point. On the present account,
Freud's decision not to bracket the concept of a fundamental
transposition is just that: a decision and not a logical necessity.

Now one virtue of a systematic approach to Freud is,
oddly enough, that it sometimes encourages a more faithful
and less reductive description. When this occurs we have a
prize case of the systematic approach's commending itself by
its ability to subsume the alternative method and to do that
method's job more effectively than it itself had been able to.
Specifically, we may say that the systematic approach encourages one to describe and appreciate the interaction of primary
and secondary processes as a phenomenon, in its own right. [34]
It accomplishes this precisely because it presses the systematic question of the purpose or principle which is being served.
For, pressing that question self-consciously, the approach distinguishes it from another question, that of the alleged nature of the activities involved. Perhaps Freud did hold that
in the last analysis the human psyche is by nature primary
process; but that is a quasi-metaphysical contention, and an
approach which distinguishes the inductive searching out of

principles as a task to be conducted self-consciously, in its
own right, will help us to appreciate that short of that es-
chatological last analysis, a certain complexity persists. [35]

A dialectical approach to Ricoeur's previous chapter
suggested that the concepts of the ego and of an "énergétique"
were indices of an interaction between primary and secondary
processes, and thereby of a heightened autonomy of the unconscious. [36] The term "énergétique" may now serve as a
bridge between that discussion and our present task. [37] In
Ricoeur's present chapter the term is frequently set in contrast to another, the term "topique" (e. g. 115; cf. 90); more
exactly, it is set in contrast to one sense of "topique," the
sense indicated by Ricoeur when he speaks of "la topique ...
sous sa forme statique, proprement topographique" (99).
Now if, with the qualification just noted, we take "topique"
versus "énergétique" as our guide, we are led by Ricoeur's
text to other contrasts which seem to be roughly correlative,
namely static versus dynamic (99, 115) and spatial versus
temporal (109-111).   Tentative as these correlations are, the
categories have a suggestive effect when they are applied to
Ricoeur's account of the three stages in Freud's Chapter
VII. [38] The sequence is no longer seen simply in the light
of a single figure, the primary process; rather, it displays
itself as a categorical spectrum, ranging from atemporality
("La topique est le lieu qui figure le 'hors le temps'" p. 111)
through temporality to a full-blown "énergétique" ("il faut
remplacer les lieux par des processus," p. 115).   In effect,
we pick up another correlative contrast: stage one versus
stage three.   Moreover the sequence starts to look like a
development--in the sense, at least, that it is the third stage
which is the most interesting and complex.   The conceptual
center of gravity thus begins to shift away from the second
stage, where it was put by the descriptive account.   Add,
finally, the fact that the sequence is a progression from the
timeless depths of the unconscious to "les rapports aux fron-
tières du système" (115), and one finds that one's attention
has been drawn rather firmly to the primary process and the
secondary processes, in their interaction.

These textual reflections open the way for an alternative, substantive response to the threat of Occam's razor.
For our observations bring to light the fact that the descriptive account tends to share with the view which it attempts
to refute a conception of the unconscious as a relatively
simple system.   Simple, that is, relative to an alternative
conception which we may evoke, not by refusing the analogy

of translation (cf. 96f.), but by elaborating upon it. It is as
if there were a coded message, yes. But it is also as if the
one who coded it--the spy, let us say--were constantly able
to alter the master code; and it is as if the spy were somehow able to observe the counterspy's efforts at decoding, and
were able to make his alterations in anticipation of those efforts. Assume a situation like that and then imagine how it
is for the counterspy, i. e. for the interpreter of the dream,
whether the dreamer's own consciousness or the analyst,
Freud. He has to anticipate his opponent's anticipations; that
is, he has to try to foresee the moves his opponent will make
to elude discovery. In so doing the interpreter will rely
heavily upon constructs of two sorts: hypotheses about the
sort of thing which his opponent is likely to be hiding and
generalizations about the types of moves which his opponent
has often made in the past. I would venture to suggest that
much of Freud's "langage de force" is this latter sort of
construct. In its specifics it amounts to a number of clues
for second-guessing the unconscious; and in its more general
nature--in the fact that there is a "langage de force" at all--
it corresponds to the unconsciousness' peculiar wiliness.

    If this be so, there is irony in it. For it would mean
that the vocabulary which is most suggestive of machine-like
operations does not simply correspond to some lower function,
does not correspond to "l'homme en tant qu'il a été et reste
Chose" as Ricoeur himself concludes (119, emphasis Ricoeur's),
but corresponds rather to the interaction of higher and lower
processes, and specifically to the interaction of a wary censor and an insistent primary process. Constant attentiveness
to the peculiar interaction between primary and secondary
processes is thus the best guarantor of that link between two
divergent vocabularies which constitutes Freud's peculiar hermeneutic; but this is not because each vocabulary corresponds
to one of the processes. It follows that there is a sense in
which our Scylla and Charybdis of reductionism and revisionism emerge as secret sharers. For to the extent that a
commentary does succumb to the descriptive fallacy of assuming a one-to-one correspondence between each vocabulary
and a process, the commentator is being more reductionist
than is Freud himself; and having obscured the genuine sophistication which Freud actually does have, he lays the
theory open to the facile sophistication of certain revisionist
critics. This, again, is the sort of point which is made by
a dialectical interpretation.

c. The "Papers on Metapsychology"[39]

Our commentary on Ricoeur's second chapter stresses
the centrality in Freud of a certain fundamental transposition,
distortion or "figuration." Ricoeur remarked at that time
that "la figuration fait problème et Freud a construit toute
une métapsychologie de la régression pour en rendre compte"
(107). Now Ricoeur's third chapter deals, precisely, with
Freud's "Papers on Metapsychology." It thus stands in the
closest logical relationship with the preceding chapter, and
with the points stressed within that chapter.

The two sections of Ricoeur's chapter represent two
complementary movements of thought within the field opened
up by Freud's postulate of a fundamental transposition.[40] I
propose to discuss these movements or moments separately.
Much of the first section consists of Ricoeur's own reconstruction of the logic which led Freud to postulate what is
perhaps the key concept of his "langage de force," namely
the concept of "pulsion," in French--in English, "instinct"
or "drive" (122-26). This reconstruction will give us a
chance to check and perhaps to elaborate the reconstruction
which we ourselves attempted in the analogy of spy and
counterspy. We may proceed by summarizing Ricoeur's reconstruction, with special attention to the role of secondary
processes; by offering some reflections on the nature of the
progression; and then by noting, as a sort of appendix, the
points at which certain newly-introduced terms seem to fit
within the steps which Ricoeur has discerned. In the present
case, even more than in the commentaries on the chapters
which have gone before, my intent will be to contradict only
that in Ricoeur which tends to obscure certain implications
already present within his own remarks.

The three stages of Ricoeur's reconstruction (122ff.)
are a progressive conquest of the notion of instinct or drive.
At the first, most purely descriptive stage, the entire concept of the unconscious is hardly more than a summary transcription of certain clinical phenomena.

> Au départ, en effet, la qualité inconsciente ... dé-
> signe seulement l'attribut de ce qui a disparu, mais
> peut apparaître à nouveau ... (122)

That which has disappeared and that which may appear again
are presumed to be one and the same: it is assumed that
the missing element is unaffected by its sojourn in the un-

conscious. Accordingly the unconscious itself is conceived as an inert and featureless limbo, a simple repository for that which has temporarily disappeared from view.

With the second stage there is set in motion a logic which will propel Freud far beyond such simple description. The turning point comes when clinical experience leads to "la notion de 'pensées' (Gedanken) exclues de la conscience par des forces qui en barrent l'accès" (123). Now of this logical turning point, what Ricoeur emphasizes, in keeping with his theme of "sens" and "force," is that:

> ... il y a des lieux, parce qu'il y a des relations d'exclusion qui sont des relations de force (résistance, défense, interdiction). (123, emphasis Ricoeur's)

Which is perfectly true. But we, for our own part, may emphasize the correlative fact, which is equally true, that it is force as exercised by a secondary process, specifically the censor: "... c'est la barre qui fait la topique" (124). Finally, this stage like the stage before is closely linked to conscious observation. So close is the link indeed that, for all the talk about "force," the stage remains a pure case of one usage of "langage de sens":

> C'est à ce niveau que la justification de l'inconscient prend un caractère de nécessité scientifique: le texte de la conscience est un texte lacunaire, tronqué; admettre l'inconscient équivaut à un travail d'interpolation qui introduit sens et cohérence dans le texte. [41]

This is the stage at which the translation analogy would indeed be valid. Dream interpretation, for example, would be a matter of proposing modest, "scientific" hypotheses, which hypotheses would be no more than a means of converting a manifest, irregular text into a text which was "latent" and coherent.

The logical movement which was initiated in the second stage is secured in the third. Ricoeur notes that once again the impetus comes from clinical experience: in this case "le travail du rêve, son activité de 'transposition' ou 'distorsion'" (123). This is to observe that not only do elements disappear, as was noted in the first stage, and not only are they sometimes held captive in that absent state, as we noted in

the second, but also they are altered, and altered in a peculiar manner. To account for this alteration, the notion of
agency must be extended beyond the act of simply allowing
and disallowing passage from the unconscious; and accordingly
the attribution of agency must be extended beyond the portal.
Further, to account for the fact that the alterations seem to
follow some pattern, one must attribute a certain lawfulness
to this activity or agency. And finally, in recognition of the
odd character and evasiveness of the alterations, one must
suppose that the pertinent laws are somewhat different from
those which may be observed in conscious activity. The manner of the unconscious is not the manner of conscious memory; one must accord the unconscious "une légalité propre."42
One must acknowledge that in speaking of "unconscious laws"
we do not simply name a place in which laws happen to
operate; we refer in addition to something we may not fully
understand, a certain oddity about the laws themselves.
With this recognition, Ricoeur's reconstruction of psychoanalytic reasoning attains a far point of systematic elaboration, a point antipodal to the descriptive modesty of the initial stage. By way of comment, we may simply note that
even at this furthest point of his reconstruction, Ricoeur's
referent is not sheerly primary process, not some naked
drive or instinct, but again the interaction of primary and
secondary processes. The alteration is the result of the
sort of negotiation between censor and drive--what would
arouse too much anxiety? what could slip through?--which
we summarized in the figure of the wary spy.

          More generally, there is something rather surprising
about this entire progression. One understood that it was to
be an effort to find a fundamental stuff, "une base énergétique,"43 which would then serve, if I may mix my metaphors,
as the archimedian point for a copernican revolution:

          ... le retournement n'est achevé que lorsque nous
          posons la pulsion (Trieb) comme concept fondamen-
          tal (Grundbegriff) dont tout le reste est compris
          comme le destin (Schicksal). (126)

Given these expectations, it may be rather surprising (to
someone, at least, who is unfamiliar with the history of
science) that the fundamental "stuff" turns out in the end to
be a very formal concept: "la pulsion en effet est comme
la chose du kantisme--le transcendantal = X."44 Now of this
result Ricoeur emphasizes one aspect, namely the fact that
therefore, concretely, "la pulsion ... n'est jamais atteinte

que dans ce qui l'indique et la représente" (121); so that
while Freud's constructs do go beyond the first, descriptive
stage and become "anti-phenomenological, " (126, 137) they
still are not arbitrary. But if we look at the same result
not from the point of view of method, whether descriptive or
"anti-phenomenological, " but from the point of view of systematic result, we also find that, to paraphrase Ricoeur, a
drive or instinct is never attained except in its interaction
with secondary processes. And when one does try to conceive of it apart from that interaction, one emerges with a
legitimate but very formal abstraction. 45

      In his chapter on the "Papers on Metapsychology, "
Ricoeur has found his archimedean point. The point lies at
"la flexion du désir et du langage, " at "la soudure du 'naturel' et du 'signifiant'"; and as we noted in our Introduction
this point is the central concern of his "archeology of the
subject. "46 Further, it is the point to which he refers in
saying, much later in his "Analytique":

            Nous avions pu dire que c'est finalement dans le
            rapport entre la pulsion, comme premier concept
            énergétique, et la présentation de pulsion, comme
            premier concept herméneutique, que réside la
            spécificité du discours analytique, lequel unit les
            deux univers de la force et du sens dans une sé-
            mantique du désir. (255, emphasis mine)

It is important to appreciate, however, that the crucial balance between "la pulsion" and "la présentation de pulsion" is
possible only by virtue of an antecedent balance within each
concept individually considered. Individual consideration was
given to the concept of "pulsion" (instinct or driven) in the
first section of Ricoeur's present chapter, which we have
just discussed; we noted the balance which was tacitly
achieved by allowing that pure "pulsion" or pure primary
process could be conceived of apart from the interaction of
primary and secondary processes, but that, so conceived, it
would be no more than an abstraction--or no more than "a
condition for the possibility" of that interaction. The second
section of Ricoeur's chapter amounts to a similar study of
"présentation" (in English, "representation"). 47 Our own
task in commenting on that section will be analogous to our
task in the previous section: to delineate the concept's internal equilibrium.

      The section turns upon the distinction between idea

and affect (in French, between "représentation" and "affect";
in German, between "Vorstellung" and "Affekt"; 145). The
balance sought here is not between these terms per se, however, so much as between their independence of one another,
on the one hand, and their interdependence on the other. If
their interdependence dominates the "langage de force" becomes dispensable, i. e. it becomes subject to direct and total translation into the "langage de sens"; and if their mutual
independence predominates, the "langage de force" becomes
arbitrary--senseless. The balance between these alternatives
is struck by saying, to put the matter figuratively, that an
affect can choose among various ideas and that it can always
choose anew, but that it can never simply abstain from making a choice (151-3). Thus no particular alliance between
affect and idea is ever anything more than provisional; but if
an affect does dissolve one alliance, it does so at the price
of becoming "un affect à la recherche d'un nouveau support
représentatif qui lui frayera la voie de la conscience" (149).

     Such is the balance which comes to be embodied with-
in the concept of representation ("présentation" or "Repräsen-
tanz"). Now there are parallels between the logic of this
"premier concept herméneutique" and that of drive or instinct,
the "premier concept énergétique" (255). We have seen that
the concept of drive was posed, by an apparent necessity of
thought, as a borderline concept lying between, and mediating
between, "le psychique" and "le somatique":

     ... la pulsion elle-même présente, exprime, le
     corps dans l'âme, sur le plan psychique (in die
     Seele). C'est un postulat, peut-être le plus fonda-
     mental de la psychanalyse, celui qui la qualifie
     comme psycho-analyse. (140)

Representation is similarly a borderline concept, lying between the drive itself and various ideas[48]--between the deepest recesses of the unconscious and that which is able to
come to consciousness. And like the concept of drive, representation is posed by an apparent necessity of thought.

     Cette fonction de Repräsentanz est certainement un
     postulat; Freud n'en donne aucune preuve; il se la
     donne, comme ce qui permet de transcrire l'incon-
     scient en conscient et de les tenir ensemble pour
     des modalités psychique comparables ... (139).

Because of the link forged in the concept of representation,

it is possible to carry on the activity in which Freud is en-
gaged, an interpretative movement between the unconscious
and the conscious (138). One might say that it is representation which qualifies that activity as psycho-analysis.

Thus there are indeed parallels between the concepts
of drive and representation; and also there is a rather neat
line of communication from drive to representation and then
from representation to various ideas. [49] But useful as they
are in placing the concepts relative to one another, these observations do not bring us to the internal balance which is
peculiar to the concept of representation. We draw nearer
that point if we raise a question which Ricoeur does not
press, the question not of what representation does, but of
what it actually is.   Is it in fact a function performed by an
affect--and thus, more fundamentally, by the drive--in selecting a particular idea?   Or is it some tertium quid, a further entity set between the drive and the idea?   In conformity
with the latter alternative, Ricoeur speaks of "quelque chose
de psychique qui 'présente la pulsion'" (138); but we have also seen that he can say that "la pulsion elle-même présente"
(140).   The judicious solution, more implied than announced
in Ricoeur, seems to be to concede the necessity of multi-
plying entities, but not to pose an entity which is entirely independent of another entity which has already been acknowledged, namely the drive.   Or, stated in terms of the other
option, the solution is to cut as closely to calling representation a function as one can without attributing to the drive
itself so secondary a process as that of selecting.   To summarize aphoristically: representation is not merely a function, but it is no more than a functionary. [50]

It is this solution, embodied in the concept of repre-
sentation--a solution made secure not by its intrinsic coherence so much as by its necessity--which supplies the
needed balance between the interdependence of affect and idea
on the one hand and their mutual independence on the other.
And it is that balance within the concept of representation,
plus the balance which we noted earlier within the concept of
drive or instinct, which make possible the balance between
those two concepts.   We noted in our commentary on the
first section of Ricoeur's present chapter that a drive or instinct may be conceived of in isolation, but that, so conceived,
it is no more than an abstraction or kantian idea.   It follows
that an instinct or drive requires--not simply for its expression in consciousness, but for its concrete realization even
within the unconscious--an interaction with secondary proces-

ses, such as are present in representation. And we have
recently seen that representation, for its part, is no more
than a functionary--a sort of envoy who may have a certain
leeway to negotiate particular conditions, but who is guided
in all things by the mandate given him by the drive or instinct. Thus it is that by their very natures the two concepts require one another.

        These reflections, in their turn, make a gratifying fit
with our earlier commentaries on Ricoeur. In effect, Freud's
metapsychological essays accomplish the task which we ourselves anticipated in the metaphor of spy and counterspy:
the essays give a theoretical framework and justification for
the fundamental transposition or figuration which Freud postulated in The Interpretation of Dreams. To quote Ricoeur
once again, "la figuration fait problème et Freud a construit
toute une métapsychologie de la régression pour en rendre
compte" (107). Now the transposition or figuration is, as we
have remarked, the cornerstone of Freud's "discours mixte"
and of Ricoeur's "archeology of the subject."[51] It follows
that by being the supports of that cornerstone, the essays
become the theoretical justification of those activities as well.
This is what is meant in speaking of instinct or drive as the
"premier concept énergétique" and of representation as the
"premier concept herméneutique" (255).

        At the same time, our tentative metaphor of spy and
counterspy (first cousin of the more recent metaphor of the
functionary or envoy) may give us some assurance that all
of this finely balanced theory does not simply hang in the air.
The metaphor suggests that if Freud the theorist wedded primary and secondary processes, it is because Freud the prac-
ticing analyst never came upon a primary process in isolation; Freud's elaborate balance is, in fact, the mark of his
theoretical modesty. And there is an important sense in
which his very "langage de force" simply refers to the actual
opacity which manifest symptoms acquire by virtue of the interaction of primary and secondary processes--by virtue of
the wiliness of the spy.[52] The contribution of the metaphor,
then, is to relate Freud's constructs back to their clinical
context, and thus to show their logical necessity. But the
precondition for making that vital connection--the precondition which virtually defines the notion of the spy--is that one
look at primary and secondary processes in their interaction.

        In light of these reflections, the concluding pages of
Ricoeur's third chapter, which are also the concluding pages

of his treatment of the first topography, are cause for some dismay. Ricoeur begins his conclusion by simply reintroducing the will-o'-the-wisp notion of an autonomous affect (149). The very idea is a shade of the long-abandoned "Project for a Scientific Psychology" with its hypothesis of a free-flowing energy. Certainly that idea still has its purposes, which it serves in the role of the concept of primary process; and certainly Ricoeur shows that there are in fact limitations upon the affect's actual independence. [53] But we have seen that the concept of pure drive or pure primary process, which concept must lie behind any notion of a radically independent affect, [54] is an abstraction or a kantian idea. To couch one's summary of an entire chapter or division in terms of what has befallen an abstraction of that sort is to confine discussion to a rudimentary level. Specifically, it is to confine the discussion to de facto terms. As Ricoeur puts the matter, it happens that in point of fact Freud's concept of affect always did retain a certain bond, however tenuous, with ideas or "représentations" (152-3). And as our own reflections of a moment ago would suggest, the price which Ricoeur pays for leaving the discussion at this level is that Freud's particular conclusions, his particular balance, are divested of all logical necessity. The door swings wide to speculation. Perhaps Freud was just being overly cautious. Why not dispense with the bond? Or perhaps he was still being overly mechanistic. Why not suppose that if he himself had evolved to the point of affirming a certain bond, his theory ought to be developed further still? Once again Freud's peculiar decision seems no more than a peculiar decision. Once again reductionism and revisionism appear as secret sharers.

        In criticism of Ricoeur's concluding pages we must say emphatically that the autonomy of affect is not the autonomy of the unconscious. So true is this that the decrease of the one may actually signal the increase of the other. An autonomous affect would move freely toward expression or discharge. But it would also move directly, which is to say that its movement would be as mechanical--and thus as predictable--as the course of an electric current. In principle the independent affect would have no independence of the predictions of the conscious observer. It would be "auto-nomous" in the root sense that it would follow its own law unimpeded; but that law would be entirely public. The autonomy of the unconscious in contrast is predicated upon, precisely, the partial inhibition of the free flow of affect. Through this sort of caution the uncon-

scious, as an interaction of primary and secondary processes, is able to keep one step ahead of the conscious interpreter, or at least it can try to do so; and thus it attains
to an autonomy which is limited but higher. We have spoken
in this connection of a "cybernetic" autonomy; we might
speak more generally of a functional autonomy as opposed to
a physical autonomy. This is the distinction which Ricoeur's
own conclusion has obscured. Which sort of autonomy is he
speaking of in the following passage, for example?

> ... le langage de la force est à jamais invincible
> au langage du sens. Nous ne disions pas autre
> chose à la fin des chapitres précédents, lorsque
> nous posions que la topique et sa naïveté natural-
> iste conviennent à l'essence même du désir en tant
> qu' 'il est indestructible,' 'immortel,' c'est-à-dire
> toujours préalable au langage et à la culture. 55

Our commentary on Ricoeur's first chapter distinguished the two possible senses of "autonomy." Our commentary on the second chapter suggested a logic whereby
the notion of the unconscious might be evolving from the one
sense of autonomy to the other. Now our commentary on
the third chapter has sought to show that Freud himself, in
his metapsychology, has consecrated that evolution.

II. THE SECOND TOPOGRAPHY:
Id, ego & superego[56]

The first topography has laid the foundations of the
freudian epistemology (159). Those foundations will stand
unchallenged until the appearance of the death instinct and
thus until the introduction of the third topography (71). It
follows that, for all its incidental interest, [57] the second topography will be of secondary importance to the reader who,
like ourselves, is most interested in the foundations. Our
commentary will try to show how this is so and to place the
second topography in relation to the topographies which precede and follow it. The commentary will thus amount to a
brief discussion of the reason why a longer discussion is not
required.

Ricoeur makes three notable claims for the topography.
It accomplishes "un certain déplacement du centre de gravité
de l'interprétation du refoulé vers le refoulant" (178); it introduces the social dimension of experience (178-80); and it

sets forth a new "économique, " indeed "une économique d'un nouveau genre" (160). I propose to argue that on the first count the topography is simply carrying out a line of thought which was fully prepared within the first topography; and that on the second count, the topography is simply delineating a problem which will not be met fundamentally--that is, on the level of epistemological foundations--until the coming of the third topography. Finally, I wish to suggest that the new "économique, " properly understood, does characterize rather neatly the extent, and the limitations, of the topography's achievement.

The matter of the "refoulant" relates directly to the argument which we have pursued throughout the first topography. The argument has been that the interaction of primary and secondary processes plays an important and somewhat unrecognized part in the logic of the first topography as that topography is described by Ricoeur--and "refoulant" is little more than a general term for such secondary processes. True enough, the second topography brings a shift in explicit emphasis and in theme, and it is possible that Freud himself may have become more conscious of the nature of his undertaking; such developments might provide circumstantial evidence of the importance of the line of thought to which we have called attention. But it is important to note they would not entail any basic systematic change.

As for the new appreciation of social context, Ricoeur himself acknowledges that the conflict between desire and authority is less fundamental than that between pleasure principle and the reality principle (179). Now that latter, more fundamental issue relates to the first topography by way of the conflict between primary and secondary processes;[58] and it has an important bearing upon the third topography, though Ricoeur himself has yet to explain just how this is so (259ff.). But within the second topography, the issue of the pleasure principle and the reality principle is relegated to the background. [59]   To recall this more basic issue is not to totally discount the importance of the social issue, which occupies center stage; one must concur that:

> Pour le dire brutalement, le systématique freudienne est solipsiste, alors que les situations et les relations dont parle l'analyse et qui parlent dans l'analyse sont intersubjectives. (69)

But even here there are reservations to be made. For the

topography treats this important issue from a limited perspective, namely "du point de vue de la force ou de la faib-
lesse du moi" (209); and that perspective is, "pour le dire
brutalement," solipsistic. Specifically, it is unable to account for a social bond in terms which are at one and the
same time positive and fundamental. And the reason for
this incapacity is that while the topography succeeds in al-
tering the earlier "économique," it still retains the first topography's "énergétique."

The concepts of "économique" and "énergétique" as I
understand them denote two aspects--roughly the formal and
the material aspect--of a single construct. 60 An "économique"
deals with the manner in which psychic energy is deployed:
the points of attachment or the modes of exercise. An "énergétique" treats the nature of the energy, or the variety of
energy, available to the agencies of the "économique." (The
first topography did not sharply distinguish the terms because
in that topography the one prominent agency and the basic
psychic energy were virtually identical. In effect, our commentary anticipated the distinction by stressing the role of
the censor as a second, even if secondary, agency.)

Ricoeur's third claim on behalf of the topography is
that it represents "une nouvelle situation économique" (160).
Thus the topography's innovation, which may be summarized
by the terms "id," "ego" and "superego," is in the matter
of deployment. The innovation may have some effect upon
the inherited "énergétique," indeed it would be difficult for
it not to; but it will not by itself create a new "énergétique."
To be sure, the deployment will no longer be decided "par
rapport à la libido seule," as tended to be the case in the
first topography (160). But this is only to say that the peculiar concerns of an "économique" have at last been clearly
distinguished; it is not to say that the concept of libido has
itself been reexamined "par rapport à" the new deployment
(209). To summarize, we may say then that the achievement
of the topography lies in the "économique" of id, ego and
superego, conceived less as a complete system or construct
than as a depiction of the clinical fact that "les situations et
les relations dont parle l'analyse ... sont intersubjectives"
(69); that the limitation of the topography lies in its having
preserved the inherited "énergétique" fundamentally unchanged;
and that, finally, the new "économique" may be seen as the
transcription of a datum which poses a challenge to the traditional "énergétique."61

This reading can be confirmed, I believe, by reference to the thematic question which runs throughout Ricoeur's account of the second topography, and by reference to the question's partial resolution. [62] The question is first raised by clinical observation of an ominous convergence of extremes. Descriptively speaking, the superego and the id--the "superpersonal" and the "impersonal"--seem almost as one in the unlimited and unreasoning insistence with which they besiege the embattled ego. "Une 'pathologie du devoir' est aussi instructive qu'une pathologie du désir" (185). If there is a respect in which the two act as one, might there not be a sense in which the two are one? The question which would have had to be asked in any case--how does the superego draw energy, as draw it must, from the one source available, the id?--becomes at once more subtle and more sinister: might not the descriptive convergence betray the fact that, on the systematic level, the two had struck an alliance? The possibility is enough to propel one headlong into the third topography; but for the moment Freud is content to seek a more conventional, genetic explanation. He narrows the question to a discussion of the process of "identification," on the assumption that it is through identification that the superego comes on the scene and (what is to say the same thing) gains purchase upon the energies of the id (186ff.).

The tentative solution which Freud gives to the question thus framed may be compared to the balance which was struck in the discussion of representation. [63] The concept of representation bestowed upon affect a freedom which we may speak of as being "lateral." The affect was at liberty to ally itself with any of a number of entities, but all of the eligible entities were ideas and, in this sense, all pertained to a single level. Now the concept of identification denotes attachments of an extraordinarily deep-rooted sort. In such cases, a new deployment of libido can only be effected, so Freud's proposal goes, by way of a subterranean detour--by way of the exercise of a sort of vertical freedom. The libido is retracted from the level of common ideas or objects altogether and is temporarily returned to a more primitive level, at which it attaches to the self (219-20). The freedom is limited, the retreat is only temporary. But in this balance of considerations, as in the previous balance regarding representation, a crucial leeway is gained.

Now the self is an object of a most uncommon sort and introducing primary narcissism as a primitive level of

attachment does affect one's conception of the libido. To this
extent the second topography may be said to have advanced
not only in its "économique" but in its "énergétique" as well.
But the effect is only a modification (cf. 305); and at bottom
the original concept of psychic energy is not only retained but
dramatically reinforced. For the proposal of a primary narcissism rests upon the postulate of a "libido narcissique"
which is "considérée comme réservoir d'énergie" (219-20)
and that energy itself is conceived in terms inherited from
the first topography.

> ... nos amours et nos haines sont les figures ré-
> vocables de l'amour prélevé sur le fond indiffér-
> encié du narcissisme; comme les vagues de la mer,
> ces figures peuvent être effacées, sans que le fond
> soit altéré ... (273)

To summarize once again, the present topography is
of secondary importance in the specific sense that its logic
is more fully developed than, but not fundamentally different
from, that of the first topography. In effect the evolution of
both topographies may virtually be defined by a point, the "Project," which tried systematically to minimize the difference between an "énergétique" and an "économique"--and by a single
consistent movement away from that point: the equally systematic effort to make the distinction and to highlight the "économique." The logic of the entire movement remains basically unchanged from that which Ricoeur reconstructed in discussing
the "Papers on Metapsychology" (122-27); and the result of
highlighting the "économique" is the dissonance or disparity between the development of the "économique" and the development
of the "énergétique," as I have been arguing. If that disparity
be acknowledged, and if it be recalled that, nevertheless, the
terms "économique" and "énergétique" should denote aspects of
a single construct, then it becomes evident that Freud's second
topography is the very model of thought which is in transition.

III.   THE LATE THEORY OF THE INSTINCTS:
Thanatos & Eros

That Freud's late theory of the instincts marked a major turning point in his thought appears to be the one observation on the subject which is safely beyond dispute.

> L'introduction de la pulsion de mort dans la thé-
> orie des pulsions est, au sens propre du mot, une

refonte de fond en comble.   (253, emphasis Ricoeur's)

But that fact is enough to permit us to raise once again the
question which the second topography because of the secondary character of its innovations did not permit, and thus to
return to our guiding theme.   Given this major innovation,
what is its effect upon Freud's concept of the unconscious,
and specifically upon the unconscious' autonomy?

Now despite the extent of the present innovation--and
perhaps, indeed, because of it--the issues attending that
question are analogous, I believe, to those entailed by the
other great shift in Freud's thought, namely the turn away
from the "Project" and toward the logic which, as we have
seen, presided over the development of the first and second
topographies.   Indeed I wish to suggest not only that the
present theory is linked to Freud's earlier thought by certain
analogies of form, but that it represents a distinct advance
in the explicitness with which that form is brought to the
center of concern.   Before, the logical form had to be teased
out by an indirect approach.   Now one can almost say that
the form is what the theory itself is all about!   Thus, once
overcome the strangeness of Freud's mythology, the content
of the theory, as well as the form, is fairly clear and familiar.   The result is an important confirmation of the dialectical reading of Freud.

a.   retrospect: the pleasure principle & the reality principle[64]

Ricoeur's own format gives us an occasion to prepare
the grounds for our argument.   In its opening chapter, the
present division of Ricoeur's "Analytique" sets the stage for
the mythic polarity which will dominate Freud's late theory
by recapitulating the evolution of the most fundamental of the
many polarities which have been woven through the previous
topographies, namely the polarity of pleasure principle and
reality principle.   In commenting upon the chapter, we too
shall proceed with an eye in either direction.   A review
which refines the earlier discussions of primary and secondary processes should at the same time clarify the logical
form which, I have suggested, will prove central to the later
theory as well.

A chapter of review was called for at this point not
only because a lot of ground had been covered but also, I

think, because Ricoeur needed to attend to a few loose ends.
For one thing, it had become necessary to compensate for a
certain inequity in his exposition: the reality principle needed
further attention. Thus Ricoeur opens with the remark:

> Au-delà du principe de plaisir ... cela veut dire,
> en 1920: introduire la pulsion de mort dans la
> théorie des pulsions. Et pourtant, il y a toujours
> eu, dans la doctrine de Freud, un au-delà du prin-
> cipe de plaisir, lequel n'a cessé de s'appeler prin-
> cipe de réalité. (259, ellipsis Ricoeur's)

And despite the fact that the chapter heading gives equal bil-
ling to the reality principle and the pleasure principle (259),
the section titles show that it is indeed the reality principle
which consistently holds center stage (260, 267, 273). In
addition, there is perhaps a further loose end in the very concept of a "principle," which Ricoeur's chapter tends to bring
into relief. But with this suggestion we are already into
questions of the chapter's structure.

Ricoeur discerns three phases in Freud's evolution
apropos of the reality principle, and he sections his chapter
to match. The first of these sections, entitled "Principe de
réalité et 'processus secondaire'," begins with common sense
reality--"l'homme normal et le psychiatre en sont la mesure;
c'est le milieu physique et social d'adaptation" (261)--and exe-
cutes three steps which may be summarized in the terms
"process," "principle" and "system." Thus our argument
for the importance of the concept of "principle" in Freud's
evolution, as Ricoeur presents it, will be put alternatively
as an argument for the importance of the second logical step
within Ricoeur's first section.

Let us begin, then, with Ricoeur's first step and with
the concept of "process" (260-1). Of the primitive couple
"plaisir-réalité," it is the notion of pleasure which is first
dislodged from the level of common sense. The impetus
comes with the discovery that the pursuit of pleasure, even
at the most fundamental level--and indeed particularly at that
level--is not as simple or ingenuous a matter as one might
common-sensically suppose. Pleasure, or rather the pursuit
of pleasure, is actively productive; it is the source of delusive
fantasies (261). This discovery is the root of the concept of
primary process (261). Then, once the decisive shift has
been made in the notion of pleasure, "reality" follows after:
the introduction of the concept of primary process "permet,

en contrepartie, de rapprocher le principe de réalité du
processus secondaire" (261, emphasis mine).

Now I would suggest that the second step of Ricoeur's
logical sequence (261-5) may best be understood as an extended debate over the significance of the step which has
just been taken. Thus when Ricoeur says:

> Le rapport entre processus primaire et processus
> secondaire n'est pas lui-même un rapport simple;
> il révèle entre le principe de plaisir et le principe
> de réalité deux sortes de relations (262),

we may take it that the "two sorts of relations" are in turn
the products of two points of view--one of which may prove,
in the event, to be more tenable than the other. [65] The
first of these points of view belongs especially to the "Project." I do not think that it distorts matters to say that this
"Project," which is in some ways the most theoretical of
Freud's writings, is in its concept of pleasure fundamentally
descriptive. That is, it conceives of the pleasure principle
not as a principle, properly speaking, but as a straightforward description of an (imagined) state of affairs. It need
come as no surprise that, given such a supposition, this
point of view finds that no actual state of affairs lives up to
the imagined portrait, that the pleasure principle remains
therefore "une fiction didactique" (262) and that the reality
principle is adopted as a description of the actual, normal
state of things (262), the exercise of "un hédonisme calculé"
(263). For if the concept of the pleasure principle is held
to such simplicity, then any detour or indirection whatsoever
must be ascribed to another agency; and the realm of the
secondary processes will swell accordingly.

The second viewpoint makes its appearance with the
study on The Interpretation of Dreams (263f.). The essence
of this alternative view lies in its understanding of the pleasure principle not as the description of a state of affairs, but
as a second-level concept indicating a general direction, "un
sens regressif" (264, emphasis mine). In short, the principle can denote an actual condition, "le mouvement inversé
de l'appareil" (264); and it may do so regardless of the mach-
inations or interactions which may have gone into producing
the movement. This is to say, in the language of our previous commentaries, that the present viewpoint, in its usage
of the pleasure principle, has conceded the psyche a certain
complexity; that in so doing it has made room for an inter-

action of primary and secondary processes; and that in this
manner the viewpoint has won for the pleasure principle the
privilege of denoting certain (actual) operations of the unconscious' heightened autonomy. "[C'] est lui que nous suivons
sur un mode figuré, substitué, dans tous les registres du
fantasme" (264). Continuing the language of the earlier commentaries, we may say that the principle acquires thereby a
freedom of operation or application which is limited but
higher. The freedom is limited in comparison with that
which the first viewpoint imagined for the principle "considéré à l'état pur" (262); but it is higher in the specific sense
that the principle has become capable of instantiation. Now
the psychic mechanism can "résiste à la substitution du principe de réalité au principe de plaisir." (264, emphasis mine)
Thus the reality principle no longer enjoys free title to the
realm of actuality.

> De ce second point de vue ... le principe de ré-
> alité exprime plutôt la direction d'une tâche que la
> description d'un fonctionnement ordinaire. (264)

And thus the reality principle too comes to be taken seriously as a principle.

We know that in Freud's thought it was the Interpretation of Dreams and not the "Project" which represented the
wave of the future; to reapply an earlier image, the second
of the viewpoints just discussed may be understood as a logical movement away from the stationary point which the first
of the viewpoints represents. [66] This decision on Freud's
part may quite properly be understood in empirical terms:
the second viewpoint made a better fit with Freud's clinical
experience. I am simply concerned to point out that, cor-
relatively, the decision may also be understood in logical
terms: the second viewpoint more accurately articulated the
meaning of an antecedent decision, the first conceptual step,
which Freud had taken before the elaboration of either the
"Project" or the essay on dreams. [67] If this is so, then
with the present, second step Freud's logic is established; it
is adopted and articulated. The movement away from the
stationary point is fully under weigh. It is in this sense that
the second step is determinative for all that will follow, as
regards not only the pleasure principle but the reality principle as well.

> Telle est ... la conception du double fonctionnement
> de l'appareil psychique. Freud ne la modifiera pas

profondément, il ne fera qu'y ajouter. (265)

The third and final step within the present section
(265-7) is to assimilate the principles to the "grandes oppositions entre 'systèmes' (Ics, Pcs, Cs)" (265). Now the postulate of a plurality of systems derives from the observation
that the activities of reality-testing and censorship both involve
negation and may therefore be attributed to a single agency
(266). But neither reality-testing nor censorship is new with
the present step. Thus, for all its imposing terminology, the
third step brings no major change (cf. 265). Indeed, one is
tempted to say that its major contribution is to obscure the
very point which we, throughout our exposition, have been
laboring to make. For, precisely because the postulate of a
plurality of systems was first generated by firmly driving a
wedge between those activities which entail negation and those
which seem to exclude it, the distinction between systems may
be less successful than the distinction between principles in
indicating that primary process, which excludes negation, and
secondary processes, which entail negation, may importantly
interact.

The lesson of Ricoeur's first section has been that if
the pleasure principle and the reality principle are understood
as being descriptive, i. e. as portraying or postulating states
of affairs, as they were in the first viewpoint of Ricoeur's account, then the conflict between the principles will be thought
to be capable of a clearcut resolution in favor of the reality
principle; but that if the principles are rather understood as
being systematic, i. e. as denoting directions of psychic movement, as in the second viewpoint, then the pleasure principle
will prove to be "indépassable" (263, emphasis Ricoeur's).
This last term must not be understood, I believe, as indicating
a clearcut resolution in favor of the pleasure principle, though
Ricoeur sometimes indicates as much (262), but rather as affirming that the pleasure principle will never be overcome and
that the conflict will thus remain as a permanent feature of
the human self. Now the effect of Ricoeur's second section
(267f.) is to confirm the lesson of the first, and specifically
to confirm the interpretation which I would propose. It does
this by looking into a number of the writings after the essay
on dreams, writings in which the second viewpoint had clearly
become Freud's own, and showing that according to these
sources the primary process was never fully triumphant, but
neither was it ever to be rooted out (269, 270). This confirmation is the more striking because many of the writings involved are thoroughly imbued with the one perspective which

might have seemed to promise eventual deliverance from the
conflict, namely the genetic perspective, the perspective of
human maturation (268-9).

But we need to examine the logic of this confirmation
as much as its conclusions. If the conflict is tenacious, how
is that tenacity to be explained? Ricoeur's answer seems at
times to be in terms of the insatiable appetites of the primary
process, per se. He observes that "parce qu'il a voulu l'impossible, le désir a été nécessairement déçu et blessé" (270);
and he would seem to be speaking in a similar vein when he
says, in two similar contexts, that "il y a du 'mauvais infini' dans le désir" (272) and that "le 'mauvais infini' qui
l'habite l'exclut de la satisfaction" (316). But if this were
truly Ricoeur's response, it would merely beg the question;
for it does no more than reiterate the nature of primary
process. As long as there is an insatiable process, there
will be restlessness and conflict. But why is there always
such a process? Why don't the secondary processes ever
succeed in fully controlling or satisfying it, "mauvais infini"
and all?

The response which emerges upon a closer inspection
will be at once more complex and more familiar. On Ricoeur's own reckoning, the keystone of Freud's logic is the
proposition that "la pulsion a un 'but' déterminé, mais des
"objets" variables"; and Ricoeur adds that "[c]'est cette er-
rance originaire du désir qui rend durable le règne du principe de plaisir" (269). Now this crucial proposition is simply
another way of formulating the limited freedom which the
"Papers on Metapsychology" accorded to affect and summarized
in the concept of "representation. " An affect is able, in effect, to choose among ideas and to continually slip from one
idea to another. [68] This ability is the specific cause of the
"prolifération fantasmatique" which characterizes the Oedipus
complex and which is of its essence, indeed (270); and that
endless string of fantasies is, in turn, the reason that "la
crise oedipienne ... n'est pas localisée dans le temps" (270)
--that the oedipal conflict is, in effect, unending. Thus we
have an alternative explanation of the tenacity of psychic conflict. But it has been shown that the concept of "representation" denotes not any characteristic of primary process per
se, but the result of primary and secondary processes in interaction. [69] Thus the alternative is fundamentally between
distinct levels at which psychic conflict might be understood;
there is a first and a second-level interpretation of Ricoeur's
"mauvais infini. " From Ricoeur's earlier chapters and from

what in the present chapter he has taken to be central, I
think that it is clear that, certain indications notwithstanding,
it is to the second level, the level of interaction, that we
must look for the logic of Ricoeur's account.

The third and final section of the present chapter is
devoted entirely to the second topography and, like that topography, it is largely transitional in significance. By way of
commentary it may suffice to quote Ricoeur's own opening
remarks, which summarize much of the logical form with
which we have been concerned:

> ... nous gardons pour fil conducteur la discrimina-
> tion de "l'intérieur" et de "l'extérieur"; à toute
> complexité nouvelle du "monde intérieur" correspond
> alors, corrélativement, une tâche nouvelle pour le
> moi, en tant que représentant du monde extérieur.
> (273)

This summary refutes, if refutation still be needed, a possible revisionist interpretation of one of the loose ends with
which the chapter began. [70]   The fact that Ricoeur needed to
give further attention to the reality principle might have been
taken to mean that Ricoeur needed to give more credit to the
role which a recognition of that principle had played in the
development of Freud's thought.   But it has become evident
that in the logic of that thought, whether viewed diachronically or synchronically, Freud's convictions about the reality
principle were not so much the input as the derivative result;
that is to say, Freud's statements about the principle func-
tioned most frequently as conclusions, rather than as warrants
or data.   It is the pleasure principle, which leads the step;
and the developments in that principle, in turn, are the result of specific sorts of interaction between primary and secondary processes.   To this generalization there is only one
major exception, the abandonment of the "Project."   To elaborate upon an earlier image: a recognition of the role of
secondary processes per se, and in this sense a recognition
of the role of the reality principle, was decisive in severing
Freud's moorings to the stationary point which the "Project"
represented; but in the logical movement away from that
point once the moorings were cut, it was generally the
"monde intérieur," as reflected in the pleasure principle,
which called the tune. [71]

And yet this chapter of retrospect has affected our
understanding of the reality principle.   The reason, however,

has less to do with "reality" than with the very notion of a
"principle"; it has to do, in other words, with the second of
our loose ends. [72]   In distinguishing between the first and
second step (or, alternatively, in distinguishing between the
second step's two viewpoints on the first step's significance), [73]
Ricoeur distinguished "principles, " in the strict and proper
sense of that term, from "processes. "   And once the distinction was clear, the relationship between the principles and
processes was clarified as well: the principles were not the
processes, but they were about the processes.   Accordingly
there emerged two distinct levels of discourse: e. g. two distinct levels for interpreting Ricoeur's "mauvais infini. "[74]
One may align this distinction of levels with the earlier distinction between processes and principles provided that one
add immediately that the interaction of the processes, or the
results of such interaction, pertain not to the first but to the
second, or higher, level.   That is to say that the principles
are "about" the processes in the specific sense that they denote directions which may be taken not by a process in isolation, but by the entire psychic mechanism--as a result of
the interaction of processes.   It is by clarifying these matters that the present chapter has made its retrospective contribution to our understanding of Freud.

     But we had said that we would be reading the chapter
with an eye cast in each of two directions; we find that the
chapter has made a prospective contribution as well.   The
chapter has made it clear that the relationship between the
principles in Freud's thought when that thought is viewed diachronically may be of an entirely different sort than the relationship to which one becomes accustomed while taking the
synchronic view.   That is, at any given moment in the development of Freud's thought, the issue of the strength or
importance which Freud accorded each principle is a zero-
sum game.   If one grows stronger, the other declines or
succumbs by just that much; to be stronger can only mean,
to be stronger relative to the other.   But when Freud's
thought is regarded not at any one moment, but across some
period of its development, the relationship becomes quite different.   Growth in one principle may elicit in the other a
corresponding growth, "corrélativement" (273).   This is possible because the diachronic perspective highlights the fact
that a principle may grow in intention as well as in extension,
in the level or complexity of its sense as well as in the nu-
merical range of its application.   In light of this distinction
it becomes apparent that the linear interpretation of Freud's
development rests upon the unexamined premise that the di-

achronic relationship of principles will be of the same sort
as the more familiar synchronic relationship. Whether even
the alternative, dialectical reading can hold together under
the strains entailed by the late theory of the instincts--when
the period in question expands to encompass the shifts and
anomalies of that final stage of Freud's thought--is the question which Ricoeur's present chapter poses prospectively to
the chapter which will follow.

b.   revision: the death instincts & the sexual instincts[75]

      The effect of Ricoeur's chapter of review has been to
clarify the status of the reality principle.   Ricoeur's conclusion may be summarized by saying that in Freud "reality" is
not to be understood primarily as a common sense datum, but
as a principle.   At the same time that it reinforced the dictum that a development in the reality principle is generally
no more than the consequence of an antecedent development
in the pleasure principle, the chapter succeeded in elevating
the reality principle to a certain logical parity with its part-
ner by means of that common rubric of "principle."   Securing
this parity was the chapter's fundamental aim, the principal
"loose end" which it was designed to tie.

      In short the function of the chapter was to exhibit more
clearly the logical form which had emerged from the study of
Freud thus far.   Now we have said that our own purpose in
discussing the material to which we are about to turn, namely
the late theory of the instincts, is to show that this theory
"is linked to Freud's earlier thought by certain analogies of
form."   Indeed we shall argue that the late theory "represents
a distinct advance in explicitness with which that form is
brought to the center of concern."[76]   Thus by clarifying the
logical form Ricoeur's chapter has provided a sharpened
measure by which to test our emerging argument.

      With this measure in hand let us proceed to an expo-
sition of Freud's late theory, adjusting our customary outline
to the specifics of the present argument.   The first task will
be to sketch the descriptive perspective on the late theory and
specifically to indicate the conclusions to which this perspective leads regarding the consistency of Freud's thought.   Then
as usual we will shift to a systematic approach, attempting
to adduce some logical form and attempting to argue that in
light of this form the stages of Freud's thought show a deep
and important accord.   Finally our conclusion will argue that

what sets the late theory apart is indeed the heightened explicitness with which the common form of Freud's thought is
brought forth.

    In our introductory discussion of Ricoeur's defense of
Freud "against the charge of reductionism," we proposed five
typical steps which Ricoeur used quite often but seldom distinguished.[77] In the present chapter these steps are exemplified with unaccustomed clarity. The "report" with which Ricoeur begins is Freud's Beyond the Pleasure Principle. Given
that it is this essay which first introduces the concept of
death instincts, the obvious question is that which Ricoeur
poses in his opening line: "Quels sont ... les représentants
de la pulsion de mort?" (277, emphasis Ricoeur's). Accordingly the opening pages of Ricoeur's exposition become
an effort to correlate "text and construct" (277-285). But
this effort to knit together as closely as possible clues and
constructs proves in the end a blind alley. Freud's hypotheses outrun their apparent premises and Ricoeur is forced to
the conclusion that "Au-delà du principe de plaisir est le
moins herméneutique et le plus spéculatif des essais de
Freud" (277).

    To leave matters at that, however, would be to accede
to the misapprehension that psychoanalysis is, or that Freud
ever truly intended it to be, a straightforward "science
d'observation" (cf. 350-366). Ricoeur springs the exposition
from its impasse by reassessing the assumptions which the
exposition's initial steps had made about, precisely, Freud's
intent. In so doing he advances to the stage of "construct
and construct";[78] and he accomplishes an interpretative tour
de force which is characteristic of his thought at large and
specifically reminiscent of the Symbolique du mal. Ricoeur
makes it plausible that in his object's very resistance to
interpretation, in the late theory's very excesses of speculation, there may repose a positive significance. He makes it
plausible, indeed, that "ce qui est le plus suspect en cet
essai, est aussi le plus révélateur" (307).

    What then is Freud's intent? "Pourquoi la conjecture
l'emporte-t-elle sur l'interprétation ... ?" (289) Ricoeur's
reading of Beyond the Pleasure Principle is that Freud's actual intent has been to show that the pleasure principle assumes and requires a certain precondition. The essay's
movement "au-delà du principe de plaisir" is in effect a
movement "en deçà."[79] To put it metaphorically one might
say that while much of Freud's theory rested upon the pleas-

ure principle, the market-place governed by that economic
principle relied in turn upon the military protection afforded
by the city walls.   The freudian twist to this metaphor is to
add that the gravest threat lies not without but within.   The
entire psychic mechanism, pleasure principle and all, stands
in constant peril of being swept away in a torrent of "unbound, "
and thus uncontrollable, energy (283).   It is therefore a precondition of business-as-usual that psychic energy become to
some degree bound (283).   It is with this task of binding that
Freud associates the repetition compulsion (284); and that
compulsion in turn is the clue to the death instinct (285).
Thus the seemingly speculative character of Freud's conclusions may be justified by the consideration that his figure of
Thanatos embodies not a single drive, as first appeared, but
a precondition underlying, and thus affecting, the entire range
of psychic drives.   Such is the movement from the fourth to
the fifth of our typical steps. [80]

    Once this reasoning has been secured, the vindication
of Freud's death instinct threatens to succeed all too well.
From its first narrow opening the hypothesis suddenly expands
"comme un gaz auquel on laisserait toute la place pour se
détendre" (285).   Yet there remains one pocket of resistance:
"la sexualité est la grande exception dans la marche de la vie
vers la mort" (286, emphasis Ricoeur's).   Thus the descriptive account takes one final turn: a return, in effect, to the
dualism which has so consistently marked the thought of
Freud (288).   In the end the figure of Thanatos, that final
extension of the logic of an autonomous psyche, is met by an
Eros which entrenches at the level "des forces elles-mêmes"
(288, emphasis Ricoeur's) the realities of man's social nature.
In the moving words of Ricoeur's summary, "c'est toujours
avec un autre que le vivant lutte contre la mort" (287).

    Now we remarked in our Introduction that even in its
final steps Ricoeur's typical exposition of "langage de force"
and "langage de sens" remains within the context and thus
within the assumptions of a descriptive point of view. [81]   Thus
what we have been given even in that part of our reasoning
which has tended to vindicate Freud's venture into speculation
is an account of Freud which is specifically descriptive.   We
may now ask what conclusions the descriptive perspective
permits one to draw regarding continuity and development
within the freudian corpus.   Ricoeur's own conclusion to the
present section provides a response.   The continuity would
seem to lie in the fact that "Freud a toujours été dualiste"
(288).   The dynamic of freudian thought has always arisen

out of the collision of two antagonistic agencies; in certain specific ways the opposition of sexual instincts and ego-instincts anticipated the present "lutte de géants."[82] Yet the two dualisms do not coincide, for the present opposition runs deeper: it is to be found "non plus au niveau des directions, des buts, des objets, mais des forces elles-mêmes" (288, emphasis Ricoeur's). But this means that, by way of the figure of Eros, the specifically social aspect of human nature now gains a footing which it had never enjoyed before. The claim of the other person now steps forward not simply as one object among others, vying for the patronage of a fundamentally autonomous psychic energy, but rather as a force in itself, capable of contesting the other psychic forces on their own terms. Thus Freud has finally responded to the long-standing charge of solipsism (cf. 69); and in so doing he has accomodated his theory to the solicitations of common sense and surrendered some measure of the unconscious' vaunted autonomy.

Thus once again a descriptive account of one stage of Freud's thought has drifted into a linear interpretation of the development of that thought. And once again, one final time, we must resist the tug of that easier interpretation. For there is an alternative way to distribute the emphasis within the present chapter; it is a formal shift which permits the highlighting of interaction rather than of dualism; and the stress on interaction assures in turn that the late theory's main figures will be understood neither as quasi-material forces nor as sheerly fictive figures of speech but, once again, as principles. The principles are related in a duality to which interaction is not adventitious but essential. This concept of duality is at the heart of the systematic perspective; it will be the source of that perspective's alternative interpretation of the freudian development. And the concept has to recommend it its greater explanatory powers, specifically its ability to subsume the results of the earlier, descriptive point of view.

Such is our line of argument. Let us begin with the reallocation of emphasis. It is misguided to dismiss the latter two sections of Ricoeur's chapter as a mere addendum, an extended indication that the instincts delineated in the first section do happen to interact; for it is in these sections that Freud accomplishes the fundamental systematic task which was begun in the first topography and which has hung fire all during the second--namely the integration of economics and energetics. We have already remarked that while "Freud a

toujours été dualiste" (288), he has not always lodged his
various oppositions at the same level. [83] In the present context we can sharpen that observation by noting that the oppositions of the second topography in particular were at the
level of economics. Now the economic level has always tol-
erated a certain proliferation of entities; it has traditionally
played Many to the One of the "énergétique. " But Freud's
late theory proposes to overturn this tradition by subordina-
ting the role of economics to that of an "énergétique" which
itself has now become the seat of a certain multiplicity. The
effect of this revolution--outside of the sheer surprise, like
the jolting discovery of subatomic particles within what had
been thought to be the indivisible ground of all--is to lay
maximal explanatory demands upon the strictest minimum of
concepts. For if I am right in speaking of a subordination
of economics to energetics or of an integration of the two
(and that is an issue to which we are about to attend), then
it follows that the "énergétique" is being asked for the sake
of conceptual elegance to accomplish almost singlehandedly
the task which traditionally it had shared with the "économique. " The "énergétique" must account for the full variety
of the psyche and yet retain the simplicity of a single opposition; it must cover the entire explanatory field by means
of a schema no more complex than the possible permutations
of "one" and "one. " Even in these sheerly formal terms the
late theory emerges as something of a tour de force. And
the importance of the latter sections of Ricoeur's chapter
grows accordingly.

Now two terms especially prominent within these sections are "fusion" and "defusion, " or in French "intrication"
and "désintrication" (291ff.). Ricoeur says of these concepts, "ce sont assurément des concepts économiques, au
même titre que ceux d'investissement, de régression et
même de perversion" (292). This is true enough; but the
trouble with such remarks which categorize the contributions
of the late theory in either manner, as "économique" or as
"énergétique, " is that the remarks tend to obscure the late
theory's most central accomplishment, which is to have sub-
ordinated economics to energetics or to have effected an integration of the two. Yet a good part of Ricoeur's exposition
turns on categorizations of this kind. A recurrent example
is the dictum that the late theory is the discovery of an opposition "des forces elles-mêmes" (288, emphasis Ricoeur's).
The second topography already had an "énergétique" of its
own--it would make no sense to think that it could have been
without one, since "économique" and "énergétique" are as we

have observed merely correlative directions, the two sides
of a single coin[84]--and thus the late theory was hardly required in order that an "énergétique" might be provided.

It would seem to follow, then, that the late theory is
no more than a minor elaboration of the second topography,
a further insight into the id. And in a sense this too is
true enough; as Ricoeur observes, "Le nouveau dualisme ne
se substitue pas au précédent" (288), and at bottom the battle
of Eros and Thanatos is "une guerre intestine du ça" (291).
But to leave it at that, as one must so long as one works
solely within the "énergétique, " is to throw serious doubt
upon the late theory's importance within the Freudian canon.
Nor does one find a solution by simply shifting the burden of
explanation to the realm of the "économique, " as in Ricoeur's
argument that the apparatus of the late theory was necessary
in order to explain how "une guerre intestine du ça" is able
to "diffuse à partir du fonds instinctuel pour éclater dans
les parties hautes du psychisme, dans le 'sublime'" (291).
For here again the second topography can reasonably claim
to have accomplished the task already. The relation of id
to superstructure was treated at length in the discussions of
sublimation; and at crucial points in his exposition Ricoeur
himself simply refers to that earlier treatment. [85]

These efforts to characterize the achievement of
Freud's late theory rely upon the categories of the earlier
topographies, and they use those categories in the manner of
the earlier topographies. I should like to suggest that such
efforts actually tend to obscure the peculiar achievement of
the late theory, which is to have secured the integration of
the economic and energetic levels and to have done so with
a rigor and a simplicity which remains quite literally unim-
aginable so long as one persists in using the categories in
the manner of the earlier topographies. Let us see whether
this hypothesis might not prove to be a more effective way of
placing the elusive terms with which we began, the terms
"fusion" and "defusion. " We have noted that in offering a
single opposition as being fundamental to the operations of
the psyche at large, Freud had committed himself to accom-
plishing the broadest explanatory task while at the same time
holding his postulates to the strictest minimum. The logic
by which he attempted to bring this off may be sketched in
two successive steps. [86]

The first step is the suggestion that despite their pro-
found enmity, the death instinct and the sexual instinct can at

times cooperate. The premise for any such alliance is that
each of the instincts should have something to gain from the
arrangement. But gain is measured sheerly in terms of
each instinct's own peculiar goal; and thus it follows that for
cooperation to occur it is not enough that the instincts should
happen to have converged upon a single object. The goals
themselves must have become identical. [87] It is for this
reason that sadism and masochism, the classic marriages of
aggression and eroticism, should emerge as prototypical
(cf. 293). The stringency of these requirements has as its
corollary the assurance that when it does occur the cooperation will prove to be something more than casual juxtaposition, a chance alliance: it will deserve the title of "fusion."

The second step in Freud's logic may be stated as a
second-level observation. It may be said of each of the instincts that its peculiar goal entails a stance toward the act
of fusion per se, independently of the ends which may be
gained by means of that fusion. And here again the instincts
are at odds; to quote from another commentary, "La libido,
on le sait, est ... facteur de liaison (Bindung), d'union;
l'aggressivité au contraire, tend par elle-même à 'dissoudre
les rapports'." [88] It is this second-level observation which
Ricoeur effectively exploits in much of sections two and three.
We may recall from the second topography that while the conception of the superego as "représentant" of the id (222, cf.
295) did succeed somewhat in accounting for the genesis of
the superego and for that agency's peculiar intransigence, it
failed to explain one disquieting phenomenon. [89] The seemingly gratuitous cruelty of the superego, a malevolence which
threw open the abyss of melancholia, remained an enigma
within the context of the second topography (184-86). But
now in the present setting Ricoeur is able to show how sublimation and the consequent desexualisation must necessarily
entail a predominance of aggression and must do so on two
counts, or at two levels: first, simply because when the
sexual instinct has been debarred, the only energy to be had
is that of its opponent; and secondly because the very act of
defusion which is necessary in order to separate out the operations of the libido, itself favors the death instinct's peculiar
determination that all restraining ties be dissolved (295-6).
"Telle est l'effrayante découverte," Ricoeur concludes with
dramatic tremor--"la pulsion de mort elle aussi peut se sublimer" (296).

In a similar vein, Ricoeur employs the logic which we
have sketched to account for the workings of the sexual

instinct; and once again that logic makes possible an interpretation of the severity of the superego. The logic of the late theory defined the sexual instinct broadly in terms of a determination to unify "le vivant à lui-même, puis le moi à son object, enfin les individus dans les groupes toujours plus vastes" (300). This redefinition accomplishes a strange reversal by which the sexual instinct, the long-time opponent of culture, becomes culture's advocate (301). A reversal stranger still, however, is the discovery that the weapon which Eros employs in this new-found defense of culture is precisely ... the destructiveness of Thanatos! In effect the tactic is to fight fire with fire, or to negate the negative: "son arme suprême est d'user de la violence intériorisée contre la violence extériorisée; sa ruse suprême est de faire travailler la mort contre la mort" (303). This "violence intériorisée" is precisely the severity of the superego. The present account of the superego, then, is an interpretation in a rather specific sense: it presents us with a further use and significance of the severity, but it does not attempt an alternative account of the severity's origin, and in that sense it does not give us the severity itself. For that, the first account of the superego is assumed and indeed required; without that first account, the second will not work. Thus Ricoeur's two sections, and Freud's two works, are complementary indeed.[90]

Reverting now to a more formal level, it becomes possible to suggest that in the complementarity of the two accounts of the superego we have our clearest illustration of the conceptual elegance of Freud's late theory. Eros employs its own second-level proclivity for fusion to turn Thanatos' first-level violence toward Eros' first-level ends.[91] But Thanatos' tolerance of fusion never issues in surrender: sooner or later it again sets off on another foray of first-level violence. Yet even the most vehement rebellion is just further grist for the erotic mill, provided only that it too be harnessed and directed inward. In this manner Freud has succeeded in generating out of his strictly limited premises the complex tapistry of a warfare "sans résolution prévisible" (316).

It need hardly be added that in so doing he effected an unprecedented convergence of "économique" and "énergetique." Ricoeur remarks of the "sentiment de culpabilité" which is the consequence of the severity of the superego, "Ce qui fait l'extraordinaire complexité de ce sentiment, c'est que le conflit entre pulsions s'exprime par un conflit au niveau des instances" (302). A similar example is to be found in the

2: The Question of Development 137

"masochisme érogène" which afflicts the ego (295); and there are indications that the oedipal complex itself may be explainable in terms of "la grande entreprise d'Éros de lier et d'unir" (302-3). We may recall our dictum that an "énergétique" treats the nature of an energy while the "économique" deals with the manner in which it is deployed.[92] In effect the tight correspondence which we have discerned between the character of the instincts and their activities--between their (first and second level) logic and their actual emergence in the superego--is itself the integration of "énergétique" and "économique."

To summarize, our reasoning has been that the center of Freud's late theory would be that part of the theory which is responsible for its most important accomplishment. When importance is measured against Freud's long-standing systematic problems, the achievement which stands out most clearly is the integration of "économique" and "énergétique." Therefore the center of the theory must lie with the logical structure of fusion and defusion. We have seen, further, that the effect of fusion and defusion is to relate sexual instinct and death instinct in a manner which we may now call that of a duality. This is to say that the two "may interact, that they may even be in need of one another, but that in some specific sense they will finally be irreconcilable."[93] The much sought-after center of Freud's late theory may therefore be summarized in this concept of duality. We must be cautious not to wield the concept in an arbitrary manner; it can never be more than a convenient summary of the long exposition from which we have emerged. But if we can continue to think of it in that context, the concept may enable us to draw certain conclusions regarding the development of Freud's thought.

CONCLUSION

Ricoeur has remarked that "Freud a toujours été dualiste ... " (288). The generalization is useful, if only for the variety of reservations it calls forth. [94] On the basis of our study we may concur with the remark provided it be understood, first, that Freud's perennial position has been not that of a dualism properly speaking, but a duality; and secondly, that the explicitness of that formal relationship, of that duality, has varied--and generally has grown--in the course of Freud's career. [95]

Now ascribing any shape to the psyche is a chancy affair--notoriously chancy, and even at that perhaps not notorious enough. But the difficulty of ascription, so far from casting doubt upon our own delineation, may in fact serve to reinforce it. For the concept of duality takes this difficulty into consideration. Indeed it is hardly too much to say that the concept amounts to a systematic rendering of that difficulty. I wish to suggest, in other words, that the concept of duality could be generated on grounds which are almost entirely epistemological. The reasoning would run somewhat as follows.

Two guidelines seem paramount in any consideration of the unconscious. The first is simply a reminder that we have no direct access to psychic energies; we know them only in their effects. But we cannot rest content with a simple tabulation of effects; any effort to understand places us under the necessity of fashioning what theoretical constructs we can. Thus there is needed a second guideline, that any such constructs must respect the peculiar nature of the psychic sphere. This latter guideline becomes most important when one postulates not a single energy but an energetic mix, a sort of psychic collision. For at such a point it may seem entirely natural to apply a species of vector analysis and to think in terms of whether there is "more" of this energy or of that. And yet it is more than likely that such quasi-arithmetic calculations rely upon a quasi-physical model which is alien to the psyche as such.

To these relatively a priori observations one further reflection may be appended, still by way of epistemology but now speaking after the fact. Our study has repeatedly called attention to each psychic force's peculiar capacity for subverting its opponent to its own ends. It may now be the proper moment to suggest that this phenomenon is peculiar to the psychic realm as distinguished from the physical; and that it is in the face of this phenomenon of subversion that the common-sense reckoning by quasi-arithmetic means goes profoundly awry. It is simply a confusion of categories to plot the course of subversions on the basis of main force. But the incommensurability of physical metaphor and psychic affairs has so long been the war cry of the revisionist camp that, having said so much, we must add straightaway that the application of the second epistemological principle counts against the revisionist as much as against the reductionist. Subversion is a two-way street; it is not the privilege of a particular agency or principle and thus it cannot serve as, for example, an unequivocal instrument of socialization.

One finds then that the psyche is a scene of conflict, but that the conflict is not a string of blind collisions. Each party contrives incessantly to subvert the other to its own ends. The result is that without the least abatement of conflict the parties grow strangely interdependent. There is difference, indeed opposition, yet there is also an important relation--indeed an internal relation, a relation which is constitutive of each of its participants. This state of affairs may fairly be termed a duality. And thus our line of reasoning may fairly serve as an illustration of how the concept of duality can be derived from the very strictures of epistemology.

Now of the two epistemological guidelines, the first is visible throughout Ricoeur's "Lecture de Freud. " The linkage of "langage de force" to "langage de sens" is perhaps the study's most consistent theme (e. g. 76); and the theme amounts to a clear, critical insistence that one knows an energy through its effects, or in its "text. " But that theme alone cannot provide a full and sufficient understanding of psychoanalysis (cf. 350); in the last pages of his "Lecture" Ricoeur comes upon a discovery which "suffit à remettre en flux toute l'analyse des représentants de pulsion" (311, cf. 255). Here, as on page 80 before,[96] we have a passage which may determine all of one's reading of Freud. To quote it in full:

L'étonnant ce n'est pas que cette négation dérive

> par substitution de la pulsion de mort, c'est plutôt,
> en sens inverse, que la pulsion de mort soit repré-
> sentée par une fonction aussi considérable qui n'a
> rien à voir avec la destructivité, mais au contraire
> avec la symbolisation ludique, avec la création es-
> thétique et finalement avec l'épreuve de réalité elle-
> même. Cette trouvaille suffit à remettre en flux
> toute l'analyse des représentants de pulsion. La
> pulsion de mort ne se ferme pas sur la destruc-
> tivité qui en est, disions-nous, la clameur; peut-
> être s'ouvre-t-elle sur d'autres aspects du 'travail
> du négatif,' qui demeurent 'silencieux' comme elle-
> même (311).

Do such reflections imply an abatement of the psychic
conflict? Does the crisis in "toute l'analyse des représentants de pulsion" imply that the distinct "langage de sens,"
upon which that analysis rested, itself is being dissolved?
And does the fact that all this is coming to a head so late
in Ricoeur's study imply that Freud came to moderate his
position in his later years? The wording of Ricoeur's paragraph might seem to invite an affirmative response, and even
to suggest that such affirmations are the conclusions at which
the entire "Lecture" has been aimed. But the fuller perspective provided by our detailed exposition of the "Lecture"
would indicate the contrary. And the reason for this contrary
conclusion is the insistence in our exposition upon the second
of the epistemological guidelines. Our own most consistent
theme has been in effect that the conflict of psychic agencies
is not to be construed on a physical model. The agencies
are not to be thought of as enjoying some preliminary isolation, each from the other; from the very first they are to be
interpreted in terms of their interrelation. And this interrelation is not to be examined by a sort of vector analysis; one
must recognize that in psychic affairs competing agencies may
interrelate to the point of interdependence and yet emerge
with a net gain, the creation for each of a circumscribed but
higher-level autonomy. That interrelation which issues in a
heightened rather than a diminished autonomy is the process
which we have called "subversion." Once again there is
reason to suggest that the phenomenon of subversion is the
stumbling block in the path of all quasi-arithmetic calculations.
To borrow a phrase from Ricoeur, the phenomenon suffices
to "remettre en flux" all prima facie judgments regarding an
abatement of psychic conflict.

In order to gain the true sense of Ricoeur's paragraph

and indeed of his study at large, it therefore becomes important that these observations and the second epistemological
guideline, to which the observations are corollary, be taken
into consideration. Now while the first guideline is much in
evidence in the "Lecture," the second is largely implicit. It
thus becomes a question of how best to bring this second
guideline forward; and the answer would seem to lie once
again with the theme of the two languages. After all, to say
that "langage de force" is never divorced from "langage de
sens" seems very close to saying that psychic forces do not
enjoy some preliminary isolation; and to say that psychoanalytic thought is never solely a matter of "langage de sens"
seems close to saying that the psychic agencies retain a certain irreducible autonomy. But analogy is not identity; and
apparent proximities may obscure the fact that propositions
have been set in totally different contexts, deployed on totally
different planes. It therefore becomes crucially important to
say that with regard to the present issue the theme of the two
languages is fundamentally misleading. There is reason to
think, in other words, that when "toute l'analyse des représentants" is brought into question, it is not because the realities which the languages reflect are becoming reconciled,
dissolving the distinction; it is rather because the concept of
the distinction is being asked to do a job for which it isn't
suited. For even after the concepts of "langage de force"
and "langage de sens" have been extended across the full
range of distinctions unfolded in our Introduction's model argument, it still remains true that the concepts are by their
very nature descriptive. [97] An approach which looks primarily
to the languages or vocabularies involved cannot get at certain
underlying issues; indeed one must say that insofar as hermeneutics is identified with such an approach, the issues of
psychoanalysis exceed the domain suggested by Ricoeur's own
title, De l'interprétation. Instead, what is wanted in order
to extricate the issues which lie implicit within the "Lecture"
is an approach which concentrates upon systematic implications.

Our own exposition of the "Lecture" has endeavored to
be just such an approach. In the earlier part of the study
we attempted to show that a process of mutual subversion is
already implicit within Ricoeur's account of the pleasure principle and the reality principle; and we argued that subversion
was possible because also implicit within the account was the
concept of a higher-level autonomy, an autonomy conceived
on a model which is less physical than cybernetic. In the
later portion of Ricoeur's account, treating the death instincts

and the sexual instincts, the process of mutual subversion became explicit; accordingly our own study had only to underscore the importance of this development and to draw out the implications for the autonomy of the agencies.

Now if the exposition has been successful, if our reading has shed light upon the matter, then two conclusions would seem to follow. First, it would seem that there is indeed a continuity in Freud's thought: a continuity which is reflected in the process of subversion, reliant upon a higher-level autonomy and resumable in the concept of duality. In the first topography this formal continuity with the later theory is not entirely apparent. The fact is reflected in a certain lack of formal clarity, a certain pervasive ambiguity, upon which Ricoeur himself dwelt in his review of the pleasure principle and the reality principle: "[d]'un côté le principe de réalité n'est pas vraiment l'opposé du principe de plaisir, mais un détour ... "; yet at the time it appears that "à la limite, le principe de plaisir, considéré à l'état pur, est une fiction didactique" (262). We may say there is an awareness of subversion, but there is no explicit awareness that the process is mutual; thus the question of which agency "really" is subverting the other. And there is an awareness of autonomy, but not of a higher-level autonomy; thus at one moment the pleasure principle seems in imminent danger of being comprised out of existence, and at the next the reality principle seems "really" a mere epiphenomenon. The burden of our exposition was of course that a resolution of these ambiguities is implicit within the first topography; but it is only with the late theory of the instincts that the resolution swings clearly into view. Subversion is recognized as mutual; thus, for example, Ricoeur's climactic remark, "la pulsion de mort elle aussi peut se sublimer" (296). And the union of "économique" and "énergétique" insures that neither agency will appear an epiphenomenon, removed from the energetic source. In light of all this, then, a second conclusion is warranted: that by and large Freud's thinking moves toward greater explicitness with regard to the formal structures we have described.

To review the ground our Conclusion has covered: we began by clarifying the concept of duality in the light of certain a priori considerations; we then used that concept and those considerations as a means of summarizing the results of our exposition; and we drew two key conclusions from the material thus summarized. Now our second conclusion is identical to the second of the theses or "reservations" with

which we began;[98] but our first conclusion regarding continuity requires some further refinement. About the logical form
of Freud's thought, and the psychic activity or development
which that form makes possible, we have noted three distinct
though related issues.[99] There is the synchronic question of
Freud's concept of development at this or that moment in his
life; there is the diachronic question of the development of
Freud's concepts in the course of his life; and there is the
final question, the most elusive and yet the most persistent,
the peculiarity of which may perhaps be signalled by labeling
it "achronic." This is the question of the normative freudian
conception. Time and again this third question resolved into
one or the other of the previous issues; and so indeed it
should resolve, time and again. But whenever one tries to
render some normative judgment about the vexed and disputed
field of psychoanalysis, one will find, regardless of whether
one wishes to rule in favor of Freud or against him, that the
third and final question has reasserted itself.

The soundings which we took at some five points in
Freud's thought--at three stages within the first, formative
topography, at the second topography and at the late theory
of the instincts--produced in each case a picture of duality.
And when the soundings were compared to one another across
the course of Freud's thought the principal contrast was not
one of form but of increasing explicitness. Now duality implies that neither member is presently expendable; growing
explicitness implies that a position is not being abandoned but
more consciously affirmed--and it is only when these implications are taken together that one may conclude that at its very
heart the freudian position embraces and requires those recalcitrant forces which the pleasure principle and the death instincts embody so resolutely. There is then in Freud no warrant for extrapolating from his work to a facile domestication
of these powers. And the strongest evidence to this effect is
precisely the turn to the late theory of the instincts.

Ricoeur has spoken of "le caractère abstrait de la première topique et singulièrement son caractère solipsiste" (70).
In contrast the second topography was marked by its alertness
to the social dimension, "[l]a considération des rôles ou des
institutions ... " (159, emphasis Ricoeur's). But it is only
with the late theory of the instincts that the social realities
depicted in the second topography achieved an impact upon
the deepest levels of freudian thought; Ricoeur remarks of
"la forme mécaniste" of that thought that "ce n'est qu'au niveau de cette dernière théorie des pulsions qu'il est fondamen-

talement contesté" (71).   It is all the more striking, therefore, to have found that the <u>effect</u> of Freud's eventual incor-
poration of a more social perspective is not, as one might
have imagined, to produce the portrait of a psyche more
amenable to common social ends.   If anything, the themes of
conflict and uncertainty have been raised to a higher pitch.
One can only conclude, therefore, that even in his most
sweeping act of revision, Freud was not a revisionist.

GENERAL CONCLUSION

But he wishes us more than this.   To be free
is often to be lonely.   He would unite
      the unequal moieties fractured
      by our own well-meaning sense of justice,

would restore to the larger the wit and will
the smaller possesses but can only use
      for arid disputes, would give back to
      the son the mother's richness of feeling:

GENERAL CONCLUSION

Our reflections may now be collected under two broad headings. A retrospective glance will treat the implications of our study regarding the concept of mystery; a second section will then consider the bearing of these findings upon one's concept of the unconscious specifically, and some areas for further study will be sketched. In the course of these sections we shall also find ourselves reformulating in a less descriptive and more systematic manner certain concepts which were first set forth in the Introduction to our study of Freud.

a. retrospect: a reformulation of the defense against the charge of reductionism

The moment may have come for us to remove the brackets from--for us to recall to consciousness, as it were-- the suppressed memory of where our journey began. The General Introduction discussed Gabriel Marcel's concept of mystery, particularly as interpreted by H. J. Blackham:

> ... the metaphysical mystery of existence ... is not to be explored beyond the world of having but lies in the mid-region between having and being, between me and my life, between the self and the world.... The body is the kernel or the symbol of this middle region when we do not treat it as an independent reality closed upon itself, but rather as an outcrop of a submerged kingdom whose main extent lies below the surface of the water. [1]

It was proposed as the study's central hypothesis that the concept of mystery, so interpreted, underlay two key works by Paul Ricoeur, L'homme faillible and the "Lecture de Freud" in De l'interprétation. This was to suggest that the concept underlay consciousness and the unconscious, that it formed a link between the two and that it therefore suggested a way of dealing with the unconscious within a theological context.

147

The first step in implementing this proposal was to further delineate the central concept. Blackham had made a start by fixing it with reference to several pairs: "being" and "having," "self" and "world," etc. We rendered Blackham's analysis more general and perhaps more accessible by saying that the concept would require two different languages or points of view. But at this juncture a difficulty intruded itself; it was puzzling just what to make of the concept of mystery's being "between." Did it designate a no man's land? or did the two realms interpenetrate? and if neither of these, then what? Clearly our delineation was no better than preliminary; it amounted to 1) a certain rather formalized "fix" on its object, and 2) a perplexity. But even these might be enough to alert us when we were indeed on the trail of the thing; and beyond that, we would trust our cases to instruct us.

The next question was to determine just how the cases should be treated. One attractive option was simply to apply our framework, the concept of mystery, to Ricoeur's two works and then to claim, if the claim seemed plausible, that the concept had served to "illuminate" the works. But it was resolved instead that we would endeavor, so far as in us lay, to apply no preconceived framework whatsoever; we would try to proceed in an inductive manner, eliciting from the materials whatever framework was proper to them. The aim was no more than an ideal and the course threatened to prove long and tedious; but it also promised a solution which would be a good deal more firmly grounded. Thus it was determined that we should apply to Ricoeur's works only those questions which might occur to the general reader; and it was in this sense that, throughout the body of our study, the concept of mystery was suppressed.

Thus the discussion of L'homme faillible began by orienting itself in terms of Ricoeur's avowed intention, and then settled into a protracted search for the logical structure which was most basic to the work. Similarly the discussion of the "Lecture de Freud" moved from Ricoeur's intention of threading a way between reductionism and revisionism, to more general questions regarding the logic and the development of Freud's own thought. The studies of L'homme faillible and of Freud were provided with their own concluding sections and there is little need for us to recite those findings once again. We may content ourselves with a reference to those concluding sections, and to our earlier warning that our formal concepts must never be thought of in isolation from the inductive studies which are their rootage. Accordingly there

will be rather little about Ricoeur in this General Conclusion
to our study in his thought; but I would hope that there will
be a great deal of him. For our task will be to lift out the
systematic implications which we have traced within his work,
and to see where they may point us. Let us return then to
the proposal of the General Introduction to see how it stands
up in the light of our various findings.

Marcel located the concept of mystery between two
irreconcilable viewpoints or perspectives. Parallels in
L'homme faillible and the "Lecture de Freud" suggest themselves immediately, but if our study has shown anything it is
that in this matter one must proceed with caution. In
L'homme faillible the fundamental distinction, and thus the
cognate distinction, is not that of finite and infinite as might
first appear, nor even that of intellect and emotion, but the
limit-ideas of belonging and objectivity. Similarly in the
"Lecture de Freud" there is a prima facie parallel with the
distinction between "langage de force" and "langage de sens,"
but we have shown that this distinction too is not fundamental,
but simply descriptive. The freudian parallel must be sought
at a level which is less descriptive and more formal, in the
pattern of opposing principles exemplified in the pleasure
principle and the reality principle, and in the death instincts
and the sexual instincts.

Once these comparisons have been secured, it is possible to bring a further similarity to light. We observed
that the two marcellian viewpoints might express themselves
in distinct languages. Just so, in L'homme faillible one
finds each limit-idea giving rise to an extensive "framework,"
running along a horizontal axis of finite and infinite in the
case of objectivity, and along a vertical axis of intellect and
emotion in the case of belonging. As regards the Freud
study, any reference to "language" is certain to make the descriptive distinction seem all the more appropriate; but once
again the objection holds, that the distinction of languages
does not attain to the systematic level. The freudian parallel rather lies with the tactics and ruses to which the principles resort in order to gain their ends. One thinks not of
a fixed alternative language, but of the endlessly shifting code
devised by our allegorical spy. [2]

Finally one might propose a parallel with respect to
content: certainly the limit-ideas of L'homme faillible are
reminiscent of a number of marcellian pairs, particularly
"self" and "world." But once again a firm boundary is set
by the formal character of our conclusions on Freud. Any

extramural comparison of content between the Freud study and
another source would require an intramural consistency, and
we have argued that the consistency of Freud's thought does
not in fact lie at the level of manifest content. There are of
course similarities between the pleasure principle and the
death instincts, but there are similarities between the pleasure principle and the sexual instincts as well; and neither
option has the monopoly on similarities of content. This
sort of comparison is doomed from the start because it has
not taken into account the radicality of the late theory of the
instincts; specifically it ignores the fact that "c'est ... au
niveau des hypothèses les plus générales ... " that both the
theory's revolution and its continuity with Freud's earlier
thought are to be sought. [3]

        We shall have more to say shortly about the limits
which have been set by our study's formality. For the present we may be well occupied with the conclusion we have
been able to draw despite that limitation. It has become
clear that neither consciousness, as depicted in L'homme
faillible, nor the unconscious of the "Lecture de Freud" can
be contained within a single perspective. Neither is unequivocal; each in its own way embodies a two-fold point of view.
The theological pertinence of this state of affairs may now be
indicated by reference to a rich though improbable source,
Victor Preller's remarkable "reformulation" of the thought of
Thomas Aquinas. [4] Central to that reformulation is the proposition that "our knowledge of the world is entirely analogical. "[5] This critical reservation about human knowledge has
the paradoxical effect of dissolving certain positivist strictures regarding the possibilities of human nature. Preller
writes:

          We only know the nature of the intellect--the es-
          sential actuality of a man--by inference from the
          acts of the intellect. What we are is known ade-
          quately and intelligibly to God alone. ... It fol-
          lows that we do not know precisely what is going
          on 'in the mind'; there may be operations of the
          'mind' or 'soul' of which man, in his linguistic and
          conceptual self-awareness, knows nothing. Such a
          claim will have immense significance in our final
          resolution of the problem of the language of faith. [6]

This line of thought has obvious pertinence to the issue raised
by Ricoeur himself in his concluding "interrogation" entitled,
"Qu'est-ce que la réalité?"[7] Moreover it has the particular

virtue of pointing beyond Ricoeur in a direction which is specifically theological.

Now Preller's central proposition that human knowledge
is thoroughly analogical follows analytically from two other
theses which Preller also derives from Aquinas: that "[o]ur
concepts are syntactically interrelated" and that "the order of
reality is not a syntactical order."[8] But Preller finds further
warrant for the proposition in

> [t]he fact that our conceptual system leads us inev-
> itably to construct a language which is subject to a
> radical bifurcation into a 'physical-state' and a
> 'mental-state' language frame, and the fact that it
> has proved impossible to indicate coherently and in-
> telligibly how the two 'languages' are to be syntac-
> tically united....[9]

It is at this point that Preller's reasoning approaches our own
most closely. In effect Preller provides a clearly formulated
explanation of why it should be that the concept of mystery is
so closely allied with a bifurcation of viewpoints: each viewpoint delimits the other and thereby attests, not to the falsity,
but to the analogical character of any resolution short of synthesis.

Two points of clarification are in order here, and in
helping to make them our own thought may begin to repay its
debt to Preller. First, Preller's argument with regard to
the bifurcation of languages does not pretend to prove the actuality of further "operations of the 'mind' or 'soul,'" nor the
existence of a god who might see all things clearly and all
things whole. But it may be the function of a concept of mystery to make precisely this point: that what is designated is
not an object attained, but a possibility opened up. Secondly,
Preller considers the argument to be only provisional; he al-
ludes to the possibility that science may one day resolve the
"'physical-state' language system" and the "'mental-state' language system" into one harmonious mode of discourse.[10]
That achievement would not cancel the analogical character of
human language, of course; the syntactical nature of all human
language, and thus the analytic argument which follows from
it, would still obtain. But the achievement would cancel one
palpable reminder of our imperfect condition--one compelling
symbol, if you will. The effect of our own investigations is
to suggest that the chastening reminder will yet be with us
for some time to come; it may well be intrinsic to any expe-

rience which we would recognize as human. One need only
recall the manner in which the limit-idea of belonging receded
in the face of any attempt to encompass it; and the way in
which the warring principles of the unconscious drew heightened autonomy from each gesture of reconciliation.

Now there is a sense in which these reflections bring
our study to an end. We have shown that the concept of mystery is not only a thematic concern in certain works by Ricoeur (that much could have been demonstrated from his own
occasional remarks), but that, given certain important refor-
mulations, the concept informs the very logic by which the
works are structured. [11] On the strength of that logic we
have carried out our resolve to go not around Freud, but
through him; and in this sense we have reached our goal. In
another sense, however, the study cannot simply end in a par-
cel of conclusions; it has marked and tested the ground, so
that one can now proceed to dig--to carry out "an archeology
of the subject." And we have not far to seek for the questions which will lead us into that task.

b.   prospect: a reformulation of the project
     for an archeology of the subject

What are we to make of our conclusions? Can anything so formal yet be useful? Has not the concept of mystery been stretched beyond all recognition, to the point of
mystification?

I want to argue now that usefulness requires formality,
and that the concept of mystery must first be so extended if,
subsequently, it is to achieve a proper content. To carry
this argument out I shall need to turn the reflections of our
previous section on end, and to do this in three regards.
First, we shall no longer look on our study as a succession
of fields (aspects of consciousness, aspects of the unconscious), but rather as a succession of methods: theology
briefly in the General Introduction, then philosophy in the
study of L'homme faillible and perhaps on into portions of
the study on Freud, and finally psychology or psychoanalysis.
This reflective turn will enable us to raise a central question of methodology.

Secondly, we shall be looking in the opposite direction.
We shall leave off congratulating ourselves upon a successful conquest, and shall turn our eyes to home. To put the

matter less lyrically, we shall start with the furthest point
which our study has attained, the setting of freudian psychoanalysis, and with that perspective in hand we shall move
back toward the original theological context. This procedure
will enable us to press what I take to be our crucial question: how, as we return to other and perhaps more embracing methodologies, are we to preserve the specificity and the
integrity of psychoanalysis?

We shall, then, be rewinding the formal concept of
mystery, which like Ariadne's thread has been our one uniting
theme; but as we do so our eye will not be upon the general
concern but rather, somewhat anxiously, upon the specific
case. The thematic shift from "mystery" to "the unconscious"
is thus our third reversal; and the guiding question may be
restated as one of preserving the specificity and the integrity
of the unconscious.

Let us begin where Freud began, with the "Project
for a Scientific Psychology. " That essay was marked by its
determination to explain psychological phenomena in terms of
the physical or anatomical. 12 Thus the proposal was doomed
from the moment Freud became persuaded of, in Ricoeur's
words, "la genèse proprement psychique des symptômes. "13
Indeed the most striking of the several changes wrought by
The Interpretation of Dreams was this fact, that "l'appareil
psychique de l'Interprétation des Rêves fonctionne sans référ-
ence anatomique, c'est un appareil psychique.... "14 But we
ourselves have argued that the most fundamental of the several changes from the "Project" to the essay on dreams is
the recognition that pleasure and reality are to be understood
specifically as principles. 15 I think we are now in a position
to put forward a hypothesis which lies at the boundary of our
present study, but which for just that reason may begin to
set the study in a fuller context, to suggest its significance
and to point the way for further work. I wish to suggest
that Ricoeur's formulation and our own are finally one--that
the logic of the principles, namely the relation of duality, is
what characterizes the psychic as "proprement psychique. "

Our study of Freud confined itself to the role of duality in the unconscious. But when a formally similar relationship reappears in a study of consciousness as well, and when
that logical form stubbornly keeps its shape despite every effort to pack it into something less complex--and all our effort to exorcise the structural ambiguity of L'homme faillible
was an effort to do just that--then a broader generalization

seems possible. The Freud study found that a certain relationship of duality is essential to the unconscious, though the
relationship of itself does not provide the differentia and thus
cannot fully define the unconscious. Similarly the study of
L'homme faillible found that duality is essential to human consciousness, though again it is not a definition. From these
conclusions it follows that duality is essential to the psyche
at large--to the "psychique" as such. [16]

Now the usefulness of these conclusions lies in what
they contribute to the end which has always been a purpose,
and perhaps the purpose, of Ricoeur's "archeology of the subject," namely the refuting of psychoanalytic revisionism. The
perennial argument in revisionism's behalf is that Freud's
mechanistic metaphors do violence to that which is specific
to the human psyche, whence it is concluded that the metaphors must be revised in a more enlightened and humanistic
sense. But the revisionist argument invites us, indeed it
cajoles us in the name of humanity, to join its proponents in
leaving one crucial assumption unexamined: the assumption
that we already know what is specific to human psyche. In
point of fact all that we know at the outset is consciousness;
and indeed the various stripes of revisionism may be sorted
according to the various aspects of consciousness which are
driven beyond their proper range. The misfortune of revisionism in brief is that in its flight from a materialist reductionism it has precipitously taken the part for the whole,
and has become ensnared in a reductionism of another sort. [17]

Our own study has attempted to skirt this pitfall by
proceeding in a cautiously inductive manner. Insofar as it
was possible consciousness and the unconscious were treated
separately, so that the unconscious might be dealt with in its
own right before generalizations were framed. But there is
another, related aspect of our study which has served the
same end, and that is its formality; for the error of revisionism may be conceived alternatively as a premature imposition
of content. This is not to say that one's notion of the psyche
must always remain so very formal, but it is to say that the
formality stands as a test to be applied to all further propos-
als. For if our reasoning thus far has been valid, then one
can say of any further characterization of the psyche that it
must either be derived from the concept of duality, or be derived independently and inductively, as that concept was derived; and that in any case the proposed description must prove
itself consonant with the original, formal concept. If we recall that it is in the nature of duality to preclude any end to

its interaction, we can appreciate that the stipulation of con-
sonance furnishes no small safeguard; for it is the hallmark
of psychoanalytic revisionism to be weighted, in principle at
least, in the direction of an eventual cessation of psychic conflict. Thus the answers to our two thematic questions--What
possible usefulness is there in our very formal conclusions?
How are we to protect the integrity of the unconscious?--
emerge as one; and the crux of that single answer is the fact
that a _formal_ notion of the psyche can protect the _content_ of
the unconscious, and that clarity about what is specific to the
psyche can safeguard the _unconscious'_ specificity.

     To these considerations I wish to append a further pro-
posal, entirely in the hypothetical mode. This is the suggestion that the relationship between the conscious and the unconscious may also be characterized by a certain duality. It is
a mark of the authenticity of the most suggestive of the recent
alternatives to psychoanalytic revisionism--I am thinking particularly of Norman O. Brown and of the French psychoanalyst
Jacques Lacan--that they share with Freud himself a certain
exasperating ambiguity. They seem to be making metaphysical
statements, statements explanatory of the entirety of human
experience; and the metaphysical character of the statements
seems to be central to what they are doing. Yet they consistently decline to engage in strict metaphysical argument. This
ambiguity alone is probably enough to account for the extremes
of response, the flat rejection and the unquestioning disciple-
ship, which each of these figures has elicited. Our hypothesis
may carry us several steps toward resolving this state of affairs. It suggests that the insistence upon the psychoanalytic
explanation in all fields of human activity is not necessarily
as naive or as pretentious as it may seem. The pervasive-
ness of psychoanalytic explanation need not carry a claim to
explain consciousness away; it may simply be a means of
demonstrating that consciousness and the unconscious are always and everywhere interrelated. Faced with the panoply of
human activity, from the infantile to the mystic, the psychoanalyst may not be trying to explain everything, but simply to
show that the mode of explanation may profitably be _applied_
to everything, to every human act. Further, the hypothesis
suggests that these thinkers may hold not only for the consistent relatedness of consciousness and the unconscious, but
for an interrelation of a specific sort. In effect what sets
such thinkers as Brown and Lacan apart may be their common
rejection of an assumption which is shared by reductionism and
revisionism alike, the assumption that the interaction of consciousness and the unconscious must be a zero-sum game, in

which one side's gain is necessarily the other's loss. Thus
to cite one example, the vision of a consciousness and an unconscious each of which is heightened by their mutual interaction may be what lies behind Brown's enigmatic forays on
behalf of the imagination. [18]

As we bring our study to a close, however, our concern is not with the various interpreters of Freud so much
as with the task of theology. We began with the practice of
psychoanalysis; by the time we reached L'homme faillible,
and probably well before, during the efforts to formalize the
"Lecture de Freud," we were into the realm of philosophy. [19]
Thus our conclusion of a moment ago may be restated by
saying that the specificity of psychoanalysis is safeguarded
through the offices of philosophy.   To put the matter more
positively, philosophy's achievement is precisely not to translate psychoanalysis into an alien "philosophical" context, but
rather to uncover what is most fundamental to psychoanalysis
and thus to make clear the context in which the concepts may
properly be set.   The importance of such a context may be
illustrated by reference to Peter Homans' Theology After
Freud.   Homans argues that the views of Freud offered by
Reinhold Niebuhr and Paul Tillich are "abstract," bereft of
their fullest context, [20] and that the consequence when such
partial views are adopted as adequate is a series of distortions.   Moreover it is central to Homans' argument that the
distortions, once set in motion, cannot be complacently contained within the sphere of the "merely psychological"; the
price is paid in one's theology as well, and specifically in a
skewed concept of transcendence. [21]   This is to say in effect
that theology must be wary not to attempt to lay hold of the
material of psychology directly, but should draw on philosophy
as an intermediary.   Or it is to suggest more generally that
the empirical, the philosophic and the theological may be conceived as successive levels constituting a structure in which
each higher level requires the lower in order that the integrity of each may be maintained.

With this proposition we reach the far point of our
present reflections.   To carry matters further would require
another study altogether.   For the present it is enough if we
have succeeded in indicating the rationale within which our
study may find its place.

Let us note in closing that the task of our entire study of
Freud has been, in effect, to unearth the converse of Ricoeur's
dictum that:

> Dans la mesure où le principe de plaisir avait une
> signification simple, le principe de réalité était
> également sans mystère.... [22]

We have sought the logic by which the reality principle, and
indeed reality itself, could <u>gain</u> in mystery; and could do so
not in spite of the elaboration of the pleasure principle, but
precisely because of that elaboration. In this connection, Ricoeur launched his "Lecture" with an express misgiving:

> Pour le dire brutalement, la systématique freudienne
> est solipsiste, alors que les situations et les rela-
> tions dont parle l'analyse et qui parlent dans l'ana-
> lyse sont intersubjectives. [23]

Ricoeur answered his misgiving by demonstrating that "la sys-
tématique freudienne" could not be understood in sheerly intra-
psychic terms; the system itself bore reference to a larger
reality. But the question then becomes whether on freudian
grounds <u>that larger reality</u> must be considered as, so to
speak, solipsistic. On freudian grounds <u>must</u> it be what
Freud himself appears to have believed it to be, "l'abrégé
d'un monde sans dieu?"[24] Ricoeur concludes that:

> L'humeur philosophique de Freud consiste peut-être
> en ce délicat équilibre--ou ce subtil conflit?--entre
> la lucidité sans illusion et l'amour de la vie. [25]

In speaking of "l'humeur philosophique de Freud" Ricoeur once
again puts the matter accurately but in a manner which, because it does not reveal the underlying necessity, invites mis-
understanding. It is as if Freud just happened to be of that
opinion.

Our own conclusion is that this "humeur" is the experiential side of a <u>logic</u> which undergirds the whole of freudian
thought. And that by virtue of this logic Freud emerges as
neither theist nor atheist, nor indifferently agnostic--but as
the resolute guardian of a certain irreducible mystery.

> but he would have us remember most of all
> to be enthusiastic over the night,
>   not only for the sense of wonder
>   it alone has to offer, but also
>
> because it needs our love.

NOTES

General Introduction

1. Lawrence Durrell and Henry Miller, A Private Correspondence, ed. by George Wickes (New York: E. P. Dutton, 1963), p. 338.

2. For further discussion of the concept of mystery, see above, pp. 13-14.

3. It is of course understood that psychoanalysis is not coterminous with the field of psychology. However we shall occasionally speak of "psychology" in order to suggest a broad contrast between philosophy or theology and the mode of thought exemplified by freudian psychoanalysis.

4. Jacques Ellul, Hope in Time of Abandonment, trans. by C. Edward Hopkin (New York: The Seabury Press, 1973), pp. 49-50.

5. To point up this contrast, one may consult the passages from Auden above, pp. 84, 146, 157.

6. Richard Wollheim notes that "the Freud who has so successfully entered general consciousness bears little resemblance, except in gross outline, to the Freud of reality. " He adds that to a large extent professional philosophers "have accepted the prevailing travesty. " (Freud: A Collection of Critical Essays, Richard Wollheim, ed. , Garden City, N. Y. : Anchor Press, 1974), p. ix.

7. I have in mind those writings which, as Peter Homans notes, "are sometimes referred to as 'humanistic psychology' and more colloquially as the 'third force. '" In a note Homans further specifies:

   This reference is primarily to the work of Allport, Maslow, and Carl Rogers, although by implication it includes such earlier neo-Freudians as Sullivan, Horney, and Fromm and, in ego psychology, the work of Erikson as well.

   (Peter Homans, Theology After Freud, Indianapolis: Bobbs-Merrill, 1970, p. 186.)
   For our purposes it is sufficient to construct a type which depicts certain of the fundamentals of this position. The

reductionist position to which we referred earlier is of
course another such type; there the principal example
would be Freud himself--as he is conventionally understood.

8. Homans, Theology, p. 187.

9. This brief sketch may be supplemented by reference to the cri-
tiques of the neo-Freudians such as Erich Fromm in Norman
O. Brown, Life Against Death: The Psychoanalytic Meaning
of History (Middletown, CT: Wesleyan University Press,
1959), pp. 203 ff. and passim; and to the "Critique of Neo-
freudian Revisionism" in Herbert Marcuse, Eros and Civili-
zation: A Philosophical Inquiry into Freud (New York: Vin-
tage Books, 1955), pp. 217-51.

10. Homans, Theology, p. 188.

11. In 1960 Herbert Spiegelberg noted that "there is considerable
agreement" that of the younger philosophers on the French
scene "the outstanding contribution to phenomenology, both in
size and originality, has been made by Paul Ricoeur." (The
Phenomenological Movement: A Historical Introduction, The
Hague: Martinus Nijhoff, 1960, II, p. 563.) Since that time,
Ricoeur has been appointed to the chair formerly held by
Paul Tillich at the University of Chicago.

12. Ricoeur's principal contribution to the philosophy of religion is
the second volume of his Philosophie de la volonté, entitled
Finitude et culpabilité (Paris: Aubier, 1960). This volume
appears in two parts separately bound as L'homme faillible
and La symbolique du mal. Among the related fields which
he has treated recently are linguistics, history of religions
and psychoanalysis; see Ricoeur, Le conflit des interprétations: Essais d'herméneutique (Paris: Éditions du Seuil,
1969).

13. Ricoeur's remark is found in Gabriel Marcel et Karl Jaspers:
Philosophie du mystère et philosophie du paradox (Paris:
Éditions du Temps Présent, 1947), p. 13. Ricoeur's principal study of the mystery of the body is the first volume of
the Philosophie de la volonté, entitled Le volontaire et l'involontaire (Paris: Aubier, n. d.).

14. De l'interprétation: Essai sur Freud (Paris: Editions du
Seuil, 1965), pp. 65-330. Richard Wollheim remarks that
"twentieth-century philosophy has, by and large, gone on as
if Freud were a figure of only peripheral significance."
(Wollheim ed., Freud), p. ix.

15. The principal studies of Ricoeur are Don Ihde, Hermeneutic
Phenomenology: The Philosophy of Paul Ricoeur (Evanston:
Northwestern University Press, 1971) and David M. Rasmussen,

Mythic-Symbolic Language and Philosophical Anthropology: A Constructive Interpretation of the Thought of Paul Ricoeur (The Hague: Martinus Nijhoff, 1971). One need only note how few of their footnoted references to De l'interprétation actually fall within the major section, the "Lecture de Freud."

16. Le volontaire et l'involontaire, pp. 350-84.

17. Regarding the term "intellect," see below, Part 1, n. 6.

18. The secondary sources, which have already been cited, are Ihde, Philosophy and Rasmussen, Thought. The essays by Ricoeur are, respectively: "L'unité du volontaire et de l'involontaire" in the Bulletin de la société française de philosophie, Vol. XLV, No. 1 (January-March 1951), pp. 1-29, translated as "The Unity of the Voluntary and the Involuntary as a Limiting Idea" in Nathaniel Lawrence and Daniel O'Connor, ed., Readings in Existential Phenomenology (Englewood Cliffs, N.J.: Prentice-Hall, 1967), pp. 93-112; "L'antinomie de la réalité humaine et le problème de l'anthropologie philosophique" in Il Pensiero, Vol. V (1960), pp. 273-290, translated as "The Antinomy of Human Reality and the Problem of Philosophical Anthropology" in Lawrence and O'Connor, ed., Existential Phenomenology, pp. 390-402; and finally "Herméneutique des symboles et reflexion philosophique" in Archivio di Filosofia di Roma, XXXI (1961), translated as "The Hermeneutics of Symbols and Philosophical Reflection" in International Philosophical Quarterly, II (1962), pp. 191-218.

19. For an extensive bibliography one may consult Ihde, Philosophy. The volume of the Philosophie de la volonté which is still outstanding would treat the "Poétique" discussed in Le volontaire et l'involontaire, pp. 32-36.

20. For a discussion of how De l'interprétation arose from the Philosophie de la volonté, see above, pp. 85-86.

21. Ricoeur, "From Existentialism to the Philosophy of Language" (Philosophy Today, Vol. 17, No. 2-4, Summer 1973), p. 89.

22. See particularly the concluding section "Une liberté seulement humaine," Le volontaire et l'involontaire, pp. 453-56.

23. See particularly "Faillibilité et possibilité de la faute," L'homme faillible, pp. 157-62.

24. Ibid., pp. 10-12. See also La symbolique du mal, p. 26, where Ricoeur explicates his oft-quoted maxim, "le symbole donne à penser." "Partir d'un symbolisme déjà là, c'est se donner de quoi penser; mais c'est du même coup introduire une contingence radicale dans le discours." Cf. ibid., pp. 323-32.

25. *Le volontaire et l'involontaire*, p. 18; emphases Ricoeur's.
    Cf. Ricoeur's critique of Martin Heidegger and Ricoeur's con-
    sequent determination to trace a longer, more comprehensive
    path toward the heideggerian goal: "Existence et hermeneu-
    tique" in *Interpretation der Welt*, (Wurzburg: Echter-Verlag,
    1965), pp. 32-51; reprinted in Ricoeur, *Le conflit des inter-
    prétations*, pp. 7-28.

26. To supplement this discussion one may consult the commenta-
    ries of Rasmussen and Ihde.

27. M. J. Blackham, *Six Existentialist Thinkers* (London: Rout-
    ledge & Kegan Paul, 1952), p. 72; emphasis mine. Cf.
    Ricoeur, *Gabriel Marcel et Karl Jaspers*, particularly pp.
    97ff.

28. Ricoeur's articles on Husserl have been collected and trans-
    lated as *Husserl: An Analysis of His Phenomenology*, trans.
    by Edward G. Ballard and Lester E. Embree (Evanston:
    Northwestern University Press, 1967).

29. Note that it is not the case, as might first appear, that the
    distinction between the "voluntary" and the "involuntary" is
    itself analogous to the distinction between Marcel's viewpoints
    or languages.

30. *Le volontaire et l'involontaire*, p. 16; cf. Ihde, *Philosophy*,
    pp. 27ff. and Rasmussen, *Thought*, pp. 33ff.

31. *Le volontaire et l'involontaire*, pp. 350-84.

32. *Ibid.*, p. 412.

33. The spectrum is introduced in *La symbolique du mal*, pp. 11-
    17. Actually the role of the "pure symbol" is more complex
    than I have indicated. From one perspective the "pure sym-
    bol" may be classed among the "primary symbols"; from
    another perspective it is the point of transition away from the
    "primary symbols" to the "concept." Also, for simplicity's
    sake I have bracketed Ricoeur's treatment of myth.

34. This is a highly abbreviated formulation of Ricoeur's subtle
    discussion, *ibid.*, pp. 148-50.

35. *Ibid.*, p. 145ff.

36. *Le volontaire et l'involontaire*, p. 9.

37. It need hardly be remarked that in saying these terms are
    functionally similar in one respect, we are not suggesting
    that they are identical.

38. Gilles Deleuze, *Différence et répétition* (Paris: Presses Uni-

versitaires de France, 1968), p. 4; Deleuze's emphasis has
been dropped.

39. References are to the French text. However in the case of
    De l'interprétation the reader will find it fairly easy to move
    from a French passage to its English counterpart or vice-
    versa, since the two volumes are close to having the same
    number of pages and since consecutively numbered footnotes
    appear on most pages. Once a passage has been located in
    one volume, simply turn to the same page number in the
    other. This will land you in the right general area and ad-
    justment can then be made by reference to the footnotes.

40. I have in mind the feminist critique of various commonly ac-
    cepted hierarchies. In such hierarchies the subjection of
    woman has often gone hand-in-hand with the subjection of
    nature, the body and the emotions. See for example Nelle
    Morton, "Preaching the Word" in Alice L. Hageman (ed.),
    Sexist Religion & Women in the Church: No More Silence!
    (New York: Association Press, 1974), p. 40. For a dis-
    cerning treatment of Freud and feminism, one may consult
    Juliet Mitchell, Psychoanalysis and Feminism: Freud, Reich,
    Laing, and Women (New York: Random House, 1974).

41. W. H. Auden, Collected Shorter Poems 1927-1957 (New York:
    Random House, 1966), pp. 166-70.

Part 1

1. Charles Kelbley in "Translator's Introduction" to Paul Ricoeur,
    Fallible Man (Chicago: Henry Regnerly, 1965), p. xiii.

2. In Part 1 most references to L'homme faillible will be included
    parenthetically in the text.

3. Cf. Ricoeur's discussion of Heidegger noted above, General In-
    troduction, n. 25.

4. A sound introductory discussion of the concept of "intentionality"
    may be found in Richard M. Zaner, The Way of Phenomenolo-
    gy: Criticism as a Philosophical Discipline (New York: Pe-
    gasus, 1970), esp. pp. 133-74. Zaner proposes the term
    "intentiveness" as having fewer misleading connotations (p.
    215, n. 16).

5. Within the present section the shadow of Kant looms especially
    large; Ricoeur states that he will proceed:
        ... par le moyen d'une réflexion de style "transcendantal, "
        c'est-à-dire d'une réflexion qui parte non de moi, mais
        de l'objet devant moi, et de là, remonte à ses conditions
        de possibilité (25).

But if one recalls the characteristically husserlian tactic of
attaining to the noetic by way of the noematic given, one may
well suspect that there is as much Husserl as Kant even in
this definition. The mixed character of Ricoeur's method is apparent in the
very titles of Ihde's Hermeneutic Phenomenology: The
Philosophy of Paul Ricoeur and Rasmussen's Mythic-Symbolic
Language and Philosophical Anthropology: A Constructive
Interpretation of the Thought of Paul Ricoeur. In a similar
vein, see the more recent Extension of Ricoeur's Hermeneutic by Patrick L. Bourgeois (The Hague: Martinus Nijhoff,
1975).

6. Having found no more promising alternative, I propose to use
    the term "intellect" as shorthand for Ricoeur's "synthèse
    transcendantale." One must bear in mind however that in
    so doing we are not speaking of reflection as opposed to per-
    ception; both "word" and "finite perspective" are embraced
    within the "synthèse transcendantale." The intended contrast
    is rather with the will and the emotions; and it is this fact
    which the term "intellect" serves to highlight. Note also
    that one must distinguish the "synthèse transcendantale" from
    the transcendental method, which Ricoeur considers to be
    more broadly applicable.

7. "L'antinomie de la réalité humaine et le problème de l'anthro-
    pologie philosophique," Il Pensiero, V (1960), 273-90. Trans-
    lated as "The Antinomy of Human Reality and the Problem of
    Philosophical Anthropology," trans. by Daniel O'Connor in
    Readings in Existential Phenomenology, ed. by Nathaniel Law-
    rence and Daniel O'Connor (Englewood Cliffs, N.J.: Pren-
    tice-Hall, 1967), pp. 390-402. The passage regarding exam-
    ples reads as follows (p. 282, emphasis Ricoeur's):
        Je donnerai deux échantillons de ce que serait une anthro-
        pologie philosophique qui conserverait l'impulsion de la
        précompréhension pathétique et de la rigueur transcendan-
        tale:
            un exemple dans la dimension pratique
            un exemple dans la dimension affective.

8. L'homme faillible, pp. 163-64. Note however that even here in
    the Table of Contents the third sphere, that of the emotions,
    does not exhibit the same clear pattern. This observation
    might already begin to raise questions about the adequacy of
    the finite/infinite framework.

9. Rasmussen, Thought, p. 75.

10. "Kant et Husserl," Kantstudien, XLVI (September 1954), p. 57.
    The article has been translated as "Kant and Husserl" in
    Paul Ricoeur, Husserl: An Analysis of His Phenomenology,
    trans. by Edward G. Ballard and Lester E. Embree (Evans-
    ton: Northwestern University Press, 1967).

11. Ihde, Philosophy, p. 60.

12. "Phénoménologie existentielle," Encyclopédie française, XIX
    (Paris: Larousse, 1957), 10.9. The article is translated
    as "Existential Phenomenology" in Ricoeur, Husserl, pp.
    202-212. Ricoeur is speaking primarily of the early Husserl.

13. Ibid. Ricoeur's emphasis has been altered.

14. Ihde, Philosophy, p. 60.

15. Ibid., pp. 64-65.

16. Cf. ibid., p. 72.

17. Ibid., pp. 64-65, 71.

18. See above, pp. 59-76.

19. We shall return to the task of placing the conventional view af-
    ter further study. See above, pp. 54ff., 77ff.

20. See above, pp. 40ff.

21. For example, on the concrete, see Ihde, Philosophy, pp. 64-65;
    on self-consciousness, ibid., p. 79.

22. "Kant et Husserl," p. 67; emphases Ricoeur's.

23. See above, Part 1, n. 5.

24. See above, p. 31.

25. For an example of such testing see L'homme faillible, pp.
    97-99, 151ff.

26. For the sake of brevity we shall treat only the beginning and
    the end of Ricoeur's progression, the discussions of the intel-
    lect and of the emotions; we shall omit "la synthèse pratique,"
    the discussion of the will.

27. Ricoeur himself cites William Stern and Stephan Strasser in
    this connection (L'homme faillible, p. 101, n. 1.) Ihde
    speaks of the task of approximating the "lifeworld" (Philoso-
    phy, pp. 64-65.)

28. L'homme faillible, pp. 104-123; the passage in question corres-
    ponds roughly to the second section of the chapter on the
    emotions. We shall treat self-consciousness only as it re-
    lates to the emotions, and not as it bears upon Ricoeur's dis-
    cussion of the will.

29. Ibid., p. 24; emphasis Ricoeur's. See above, pp. 40-41.

30. Ibid. , p. 99; emphasis Ricoeur's. The question may be raised
     whether "... l'intention du connaître ... " is indeed intention-
     ality. Certainly the common English usage of "intention" is
     quite different from the philosophic sense of "intentionality,"
     at least as that term is employed in phenomenological cir-
     cles; and the same is true of the cognate terms in French.
     But in the present case Ricoeur's context leaves little room
     for doubt. The passage follows upon the title "Intentionnali-
     té et intimité du sentiment"; and it is followed in turn by a
     discussion of "... la relation 'horizontale' que le sentiment
     institute entre le moi et le monde ... ," p. 99.

31. Ibid.; emphasis Ricoeur's. See above, pp. 45-46.

32. Ibid. , p. 101. See above, p. 42.

33. I propose to use the term "belonging" indifferently to cover
     both modes: the subject's owning something and the subject's
     belonging to something.

34. Ibid. , p. 100; emphasis mine. That we are not unduly stres-
     sing the term, however, is evident from the title "Intention-
     nalité et intimité du sentiment," p. 99.

35. See below, Part 1, n. 71.

36. The terms "horizontal" and "vertical" have been chosen simply
     because they are of themselves fairly neutral and because
     they accord with the relationships suggested by the very shape
     of the book's Table of Contents, so that the intent is easy to
     remember. One should note, however, that our usage is
     distinct from, and roughly contrary to, Ricoeur's own (in-
     frequent) use of the same terms, pp. 99-100, 107.

37. See above, pp. 40-41.

38. See above, pp. 37-40.

39. See above, pp. 37ff.

40. See above, pp. 34-35.

41. See above, p. 36.

42. Cf. above, pp. 43-44.

43. See above, pp. 40-41.

44. L'homme faillible, p. 108. In Ricoeur's text the terms "thu-
     mos," "epithumia" and "eros" appear in Greek script and
     are italicized. In our text we transliterate the terms and
     set them apart by the use of quotes.

45. See above, Part 1, n. 6.

46. See above, p. 61.

47. See above, pp. 57-58.

48. Cf. Ihde's observation (Philosophy, pp. 62-63):
    What must be noted is that, although the order to be fol-
    lowed in the text of Fallible Man always begins with the
    finite pole prior to moving to an implied infinitude, the
    categorial schema itself is clearly weighted transcendent-
    ally. It is always the infinite focus of the dialectic which
    is privileged. The dialectic as a "deduction" is the meas-
    ured limitation of transcendence.

49. See above, pp. 37-40.

50. See above, pp. 53-54.

51. L'homme faillible, p. 97; I have altered Ricoeur's emphasis.

52. We have considered the possibility that by "intention" Ricoeur
    might mean something other than "intentionnalité"; see above,
    Part 1, n. 30.

53. L'homme faillible, p. 100; emphasis Ricoeur's.   On the para-
    dox of the emotions, see above, pp. 49ff.

54. See above, pp. 50-52.

55. On the "genèse réciproque," see above, pp. 45-47.

56. See above, pp. 66ff.

57. L'homme faillible, p. 146; emphasis mine. On "le désir du
    désir," cf. p. 143: "Une situation proprement humaine naît
    dès qu'un désir quelconque est traversé par ce désir du dé-
    sir...."

58. The exception follows upon a description of the manner in
    which the satisfactions of mere pleasure may impede one's
    progress toward true happiness. It states that pleasure is
    also finite "en un autre sens," which proves to be a quite
    positive sense (110). But this lone statement hangs in mid-
    air, having been given no connection with the surrounding
    context.

59. Note the important place accorded the term in our analysis of
    Ricoeur's style, above, p. 61.

60. L'homme faillible, p. 119; emphasis mine. On "la schémati-
    sation," cf. p. 146.

61.   The pertinent passages in our study are as follows: on the
      concepts, pp. 29ff.; on the frameworks, pp. 65ff.; on the
      models, pp. 85ff.; and for the "explication de texte," pp.
      74ff.

62.   See above, p. 44.

63.   See above, p. 53.

64.   See above, pp. 40-43.

65.   See above, pp. 47-48.

66.   See above, pp. 45-47, 63-64.

67.   See above, pp. 45ff.

68.   In one of the three crucial passages, on p. 107, the term it-
      self does not even appear; cf. pp. 99, 118.

69.   See above, p. 50.

70.   See above, pp. 53-54.

71.   Thus Ricoeur's treatment of this concept (118) may stand in
      for the discussion of objectivity which we declined to under-
      take; see above, pp. 53-54.

Part 2

1.   Following Ricoeur, I propose to use "text" to refer to any form
      of cultural expression which might be observed and thus inter-
      preted. See for example, Ricoeur, De l'interprétation, p.
      54:

         Telle est l'ultime racine de notre problème: elle réside
         dans cette connexion primitive entre l'acte d'exister et les
         signes que nous déployons dans nos oeuvres; la réflexion
         doit devenir interprétation, parce que je ne peux saisir cet
         acte d'exister ailleurs que dans les signes épars dans le
         monde.
      Regarding La symbolique du mal, see above, pp. 17-19.

2.   In the course of the present study we will frequently have occa-
      sion to distinguish levels of reasoning or interpretation. I
      think this procedure can be illuminating. It has become some-
      thing of a vogue, however, to speak of "meta-" disciplines;
      and the tenor of these proposals sometimes suggests that one
      is opening up an unexplored field--as if the primitive first-
      level practitioners had never reflected upon what they were
      about. My own proposal is simply to distinguish more clear-
      ly two sorts of activity, each of which is already under way.

3. De l'interprétation, pp. 40ff. Henceforth references to De l'in-
    terprétation in Part Two of our study will generally be in-
    cluded parenthetically in the text.

4. Cf. the study of Wilhelm Dilthey, particularly the discussion of
    "The 'Human Sciences' versus the 'Natural Sciences'" in
    Richard E. Palmer, Hermeneutics: Interpretation Theory in
    Schleiermacher, Dilthey, Heidegger, and Gadamer (Evanston:
    Northwestern University Press, 1969), pp. 103ff.

5. On the "longer path," see above, General Introduction, n. 25.

6. I have not attempted to furnish references for the numerous
    points concentrated within this model argument. Many of the
    issues may be found, however, in Ricoeur's preliminary dis-
    cussion of "le problème épistémologique du freudisme," De
    l'interprétation, pp. 75-77. For a particularly clear example
    of the model's application, see above, pp. 130-131.

7. Ibid., p. 384; emphases are mine, to highlight Ricoeur's paral-
    lelisms. On the significance of these points, see above, p.
    94.

8. On the "diagnostique," see above, pp. 15-16.

9. On the basis of such a comparison, as we note above, p. 92,
    the "langage de force" is understood to survive " . . . not
    merely as a fortuitous vestige, but as a vocabulary charged
    with a significance of its own and providing the 'langage de
    sens' with a needed complement or foil. " On the "symbol-
    ique," see above, pp. 17-19.

10. This reasoning is spelled out somewhat further in our General
    Conclusion; see above, pp. 150-52.

11. Cf. above, p. 14.

12. Sigmund Freud, The Standard Edition of the Complete Psycholog-
    ical Works of Sigmund Freud, ed. by James Strachey (London:
    Hogarth Press, 1953-), XXII, 95.

13. De l'interprétation, p. 80; emphasis mine. The quote regard-
    ing the machine is from Freud, The Origins of Psychoanaly-
    sis, trans. by Eric Mosbacher and James Strachey (New
    York: Basic Books, 1954), p. 129.

14. Regarding the revisionist interpretation of Freud, see above,
    pp. 5-7.

15. De l'interprétation, p. 384; emphasis mine. Quoted above, p.
    8.

16. See for example his critique of "the adaptive point of view,"

ibid., pp. 362-64.

17. See above, pp. 17-19.

18. See Ricoeur, La symbolique du mal, pp. 31ff.

19. But the present study will be defined by the effort to attain a
     systematic level. We shall not spend much time, therefore,
     over the finer distinctions within the descriptive level; in
     particular, it will not be a major concern of ours to assign
     various portions of Ricoeur's exposition to the various stages
     of our earlier model argument (above, pp. 86-88). For an
     example of such a sorting, however, see above, pp. 130-131.

20. Cf. David Bakan, The Duality of Human Existence: Isolation
     and Communion in Western Man (Boston: Beacon Press,
     1966). Though Bakan gives prominence to the term "duality,"
     his basic intent is indicated by the subtitle; it is in the con-
     text of the dilemmas of "agency" and "communion" that his
     particular use of "duality" is to be understood. The use of
     this same term, "duality," within the present study is purely
     coincidental.

21. De l'interprétation, p. 384; quoted above, p. 88. The passage
     from p. 54, quoted above, Part 2, n. 1, is suggestive re-
     garding the link between the "archeology" and Ricoeur's lar-
     ger philosophical concerns; similar issues are of course
     taken up in the "Dialectique," pp. 333ff.

22. De l'interprétation, p. 80; quoted above, p. 91.

23. The terminology of "synchronic" and "diachronic" is borrowed
     from Ferdinand de Saussure, Cours de linguistique génèrale,
     ed. by Charles Bally and Albert Sechehaye (Paris: Payot,
     1966), pp. 114-17.

24. On the current French scene the metaphor of archeology is
     commonly associated with the work of Michel Foucault. One
     may note however that the writings of Foucault in which the
     term is prominent have appeared subsequently to the publica-
     tion of De l'interprétation in 1965; see Les mots et les cho-
     ses: Une archéologie des sciences humaines (Paris: Édi-
     tions Gallimard, 1966) and L'archéologie du savoir (Paris:
     Éditions Gallimard, 1969).

25. De l'interprétation, pp. 79-94.

26. Freud, The Origins of Psychoanalysis, p. 355; quoted by Ri-
     coeur, De l'interprétation, p. 81.

27. De l'interprétation, p. 88, n. 24; cf. Jean Laplanche et J.-B.
     Pontalis, Vocabulaire de la psychanalyse (Paris: Presses
     Universitaires de France, 1968), p. 241.

28. Freud, The Origins of Psychoanalysis, p. 129; quoted above, p. 91.

29. Ibid.

30. Laplanche et Pontalis, Vocabulaire, pp. 341-43.

31. De l'interprétation, pp. 95-119.

32. Ibid., p. 107. On the centrality of the concept of "regression" to freudian theory, one may consult Peter Madison, Freud's Concept of Repression and Defense, Its Theoretical and Observational Language, (Minneapolis: University of Minnesota Press, 1961), esp. pp. 34-36.

33. De l'interprétation, p. 109. Ricoeur characterizes the third stage as one of "la force et le conflit"; but I take it that the latter must be the operational term, since "force" has already come upon the scene in the previous stage.

34. In calling it a "phenomenon," I do not mean to deny that the interaction is discovered by an act of interpretation; it is hardly a simple datum. The issue is whether the interaction so attained is then to be examined inductively, or "explained" on a priori grounds.

35. In the General Conclusion, with our completed study as a base, we will be able to suggest a fuller and less combative appreciation of even the apparently metaphysical aspect of Freud's thought; see above, pp. 155-156.

36. See above, pp. 101-102.

37. For further clarification of the term "énergétique," see below, Part 2, n. 45 and above, p. 118.

38. The stages are those summarized in De l'interprétation, p. 109 and above, p. 104.

39. De l'interprétation, pp. 120-153.

40. Ibid., p. 212; n. 3 is of particular interest.

41. Ibid., p. 124; cf. the third stage of our model argument, "text & construct," above p. 87.

42. De l'interprétation, p. 123; I have dropped Ricoeur's emphasis.

43. Ibid., p. 292. In a general way one may say of the present chapter in Ricoeur that its first section reflects the concerns of an "énergétique" and the second, those of an "économique."

44. Ibid., p. 121. Ricoeur's likening of his reconstructed logic to

a transcendental deduction (cf. pp. 124, 366) seems to me
plausible but inessential to his argument.

45.   In the course of the present section, Ricoeur has made frequent use of a number of terms which are bound to be rather
puzzling.   It is simply impossible to do a proper study of
each of these within the bounds of our commentary.   It may
be useful, however, to try to place some of them within the
one firm framework which Ricoeur has given us, namely the
three stages of his reconstructed logic.
Of the several terms, only one is identifiable with a single
stage.   "Dynamique, " used adjectivally, applies exclusively
to the second, transitional stage (123-4).   The other terms
are able to function substantivally; and they display a
greater versatility.
Within the concept of "topique" there are, I believe, some
three distinct themes at play.   Most conventionally, of
course, "topique" denotes that differentiation within the
concept of the psyche which results from the discovery of
another "légalité propre, " and thus of the unconscious.
On this count it corresponds to the second and third stages,
and Ricoeur can observe, "On voit ... combien sont liées
les considérations énergétiques et topiques ... " (123).
But when Ricoeur wishes to draw attention to that which
distinguishes the present topography, the first, from those
which will follow, he may use the term "topique" to suggest a certain interdependence of the key terms of that
topography--"conscious, " "unconscious, " "pre-conscious"--
which interdependence was most evident in the first stage
of his reconstructed logic (123).   Finally, the idea of a
psychic space also conveys a connotation of timelessness
which is not reminiscent of any of the present stages so
much as it is of the first of the three steps which were
distinguished in Ricoeur's previous chapter (109-113; cf.
151-2).
"Économique" and "énergétique" are both allied with that
logic which is initiated in the second stage and carried
through to the third (149).   The terms appear virtually
interchangeable, though "économique" is the more commonly used, as on the frequent occasions when "économique"
and "topique" are contrasted as comprehensive alternatives
(v. a. our commentary on the previous chapter).   I think,
however, that there is a difference of nuance which we
will do well to keep in mind.   To put it roughly, "économique" calls attention to the formal aspect, and "énergetique, "
to the material aspect, of the logic to which we referred.
To speak of setting forth an "énergétique" is to call to
mind the familiar quest for a fundamental stuff--a relatively simple theme which is constant throughout the several stages.   "Économique, " in contrast, suggests something more complex: the patterns of agency which, with
each stage, somewhat alter in purpose and effect.

46.   Ibid., p. 384; cf. above p. 94.

47.   Thus Ricoeur's chapter title "Pulsion et représentation ... "
      (120, emphasis mine) may be misleading; it again reflects a
      descriptive emphasis. On the terms "présentation" and
      "représentation" see p. 121, n. 2.

48.   Cf. the various "rejetons" (in English, the "derivatives of the
      unconscious"), pp. 152f.

49.   This line is, in effect, the "trajet inverse" described by Ri-
      coeur's second section, in contrast to the first (137, cf. 121).

50.   On this entire issue, including the metaphor of "un délégué,"
      I have drawn heavily upon the indispensable Laplanche et
      Pontalis, Vocabulaire, pp. 411f.

51.   See above, pp. 103ff.

52.   Cf. our original determination to locate "some sort of opacity,
      something reminiscent of the primitive literalism within the
      'symbolique' ... " see above, p. 94.

53.   This is the theme of points "1" and "2" of his summary, pp.
      151-53.

54.   Cf. Laplanche et Pontalis, Vocabulaire, pp. 12f.; accordingly,
      I will not at present stress the distinction between "uncon-
      scious affect" and drive or instinct, important though that
      distinction may be in other contexts.

55.   De l'interprétation, pp. 151-52. Similarly, note his remarks
      on "le désir comme désir" on p. 152, n. 81.

56.   Ibid., pp. 157-249.

57.   The topography includes some of Freud's most widely known
      terminology--id, ego, superego--and much of his cultural
      criticism.

58.   See Laplanche et Pontalis, Vocabulaire, p. 342.

59.   As regards explicit discussion, one may simply note how few
      of the entries under "pleasure principle" and "reality prin-
      ciple" in the Index to the English translation fall within the
      discussion of the second topography.

60.   See above, Part 2, n. 45.

61.   Cf. the fact that the second topography neither replaces the
      first, nor is simply added to it, De l'interprétation, p. 159.

62.   For instances of the question, see De l'interprétation, pp.

185-86, 207-10, 219-25, cf. 294; for the partial resolution, see pp. 219-25.

63. See above, pp. 111-112.

64. De l'interprétation, pp. 259-276.

65. The larger context seems to dictate this reading, as I shall try to show; I am aware that this is not the obvious sense of the words which we have quoted.

66. See above, pp. 109-110.

67. It should perhaps be added that while we have identified the viewpoints by way of two freudian writings, we ought not to identify them with those writings. Ricoeur appears to understand the viewpoints as types (262); and that they were such would explain how the first viewpoint was able to survive somewhat Freud's repudiation of the "Project." As to why a certain retention of the viewpoint was not only possible but necessary, I would suggest that it may have been only gradually that Freud came fully to distinguish primary process from the pleasure principle. In so far as that distinction had not become entirely clear, Freud might still use, or misuse, the term "pleasure principle" when a first-level concept was called for.

68. See above, pp. 111-112.

69. See above, pp. 110f.

70. See above, pp. 121f.

71. See above, p. 124.

72. See above, p. 122.

73. See above, pp. 122ff.

74. See above, pp. 126f.

75. De l'interprétation, pp. 277-303.

76. See above, p. 121.

77. See above, pp. 86-88.

78. See above, pp. 87f.

79. The phrase "en deçà" is mine; but cf. "en arrière," p. 305.

80. See above, pp. 87f.

81. See above, p. 93.

82. De l'interprétation, pp. 288-89; the phrase is Freud's.

83. See above, pp. 131f.

84. See above, Part 2, n. 45.

85. E. g. De l'interprétation, p. 295: " ... c'est le lieu de le
     repéter: le surmoi est le 'représentant du ça' (Vertreter
     des Es).

86. Our discussion draws heavily upon Laplanche et Pontalis, Vo-
     cabulaire, pp. 507-09.

87. Ibid. , p. 508.

88. Ibid. ; the quotation within the quotation is from Freud, Stand-
     ard Edition, XXIII, 148.

89. De l'interprétation, pp. 224-25; see above, p. 119.

90. Ricoeur says of the readings given by The Ego and the Id and
     Civilization and its Discontents, "Les deux lectures sont non
     seulement superposées, mais imbriquées l'une dans l'autre
     ... " (301); the same may be said of Ricoeur's second and
     third sections, which treat these essays respectively.

91. The levels spoken of here correspond to the two steps of our
     exposition of a moment ago, and thus to the issue of fusion
     and defusion, according to goal (the first level) and the is-
     sue of stance toward fusion and defusion per se, irrespective
     of goal (the second level); see above, p. 129f.

92. See above, p. 118.

93. See above, p. 94.

94. Ricoeur's own reservation is that "c'est la répartition des
     termes opposés et la nature même de l'opposition qui a sans
     cesse varié, " (288).

95. These two points simply recapitulate the theses with which we
     began our study of Freud's late theory; see above, p. 121.

96. See above, p. 91.

97. See above, p. 93.

98. See above, p. 138.

99. See above, pp. 95f.

General Conclusion

1. Blackham, Six Existentialist Thinkers, p. 72; the emphasis is
    mine.

2. See above, p. 107.

3. Ricoeur, De l'interprétation, p. 254.

4. Victor Preller, Divine Science and the Science of God: A Refor-
    mulation of Thomas Aquinas (Princeton, N. J. : Princeton
    University Press, 1967). Our purposes do not require us to
    raise the question of the extent to which Preller has been
    true to Aquinas; we may treat the work as a proposal which
    is of interest in its own right.

5. Ibid., p. 69; emphasis is mine.

6. Ibid., pp. 72-73; emphases Preller's. On the language of faith,
    see ibid., pp. 226ff.

7. Ricoeur, De l'interprétation, pp. 317ff.

8. Preller, Reformulation, p. 52.

9. Ibid., pp. 73-74; cf. pp. 59ff.

10. Ibid., p. 72.

11. Peter Homans, for example, has pointed out the thematic con-
    cern; see Theology after Freud, p. 213.

12. Ricoeur, De l'interprétation, p. 81.

13. Ibid., p. 92; cf. above, p. 103.

14. Ibid., p. 95; emphasis Ricoeur's. Cf. p. 140.

15. See above, pp. 123f.

16. It has often been proposed that the essence of the psyche, or
    at least of consciousness, may lie in intentionality. It is
    therefore appropriate to recall that our exposition of L'homme
    faillible discovered in the "genèse réciproque" a close, for-
    mative bond between intentionality and a certain duality; see
    above, pp. 70f.

17. On the criticism of freudian revisionism, see above, pp. 5-7.

18. See Norman O. Brown, Love's Body (New York: Random
    House, 1966), passim. Cf. Jacques Lacan, Écrits (Paris:
    Éditions du Seuil, 1966).

19. "... ce livre n'est pas un livre de psychologie, mais de philo-
     sophie," Ricoeur, De l'interprétation, p. 8.

20. Homans, Theology after Freud, p. 14.

21. Ibid., pp. 66-67; cf. pp. 91ff.

22. Ricoeur, De l'interprétation, p. 317.

23. Ibid., p. 69.

24. Ibid., p. 320.

25. Ibid., p. 330.

SELECTED BIBLIOGRAPHY

A detailed bibliography of the writings of Paul Ricoeur has been published by Dirk Vansina in the Revue philosophique de Louvain, Vol. LX (August 1962), and supplemented by the same author, Revue Philosophique de Louvain, Vol. LXVI (February 1968). That bibliography in turn has been reviewed by Don Ihde and a list of secondary sources has been supplied; see Don Ihde, Hermeneutic Phenomenology: The Philosophy of Paul Ricoeur, pp. 183-90. The present bibliography confines itself to an account of the works which have been central to the present study. Writings by Ricoeur are listed in chronological order.

a. By Paul Ricoeur

Gabriel Marcel et Karl Jaspers: Philosophie du mystère et philosophie du paradoxe. Paris: Temps Présent, 1948.

Philosophie de la volonté. I: Le volontaire et l'involontaire. Paris: Aubier, 1950. (English translation by Erazim Kohák. Freedom and Nature: The Voluntary and the Involuntary. Evanston, Ill. : Northwestern University Press, 1966.)

"Kant et Husserl." Kantstudien, XLVI (September 1954), 44-67. (English translation by Edward G. Ballard and Lester E. Embree. "Kant and Husserl" in Paul Ricoeur. Husserl: An Analysis of His Phenomenology. Evanston, Ill. : Northwestern University Press, 1967).

"Phénoménologie existentielle." Encyclopédie française, XIX, 10. 8-10. 12. Paris: Larousse, 1957. (English translation by Edward G. Ballard and Lester E. Embree. "Existential Phenomenology" in Paul Ricoeur. Husserl: An Analysis of His Phenomenology. Evanston, Ill. : Northwestern University Press, 1967.)

Philosophie de la volonté. Finitude et culpabilité. I: L'homme faillible. Paris: Aubier, 1960. (English translation by Charles Kelbley. Fallible Man. Chicago: Henry Regnery, 1965.) II: La symbolique du mal. Paris: Aubier, 1960. (English translation by Emerson Buchanan. The Symbolism of Evil. New York: Harper & Row, 1967.)

De l'interprétation: Essai sur Freud. Paris: Éditions du Seuil,
   1965. (English translation by Denis Savage. Freud and
   Philosophy: An Essay on Interpretation. New Haven, Conn. :
   Yale University Press, 1970.)

Entretiens, Paul Ricoeur et Gabriel Marcel. Paris: Aubier-Mon-
   taigne, 1968.

Le conflit des interprétations: Essais d'herméneutique. Paris:
   Éditions de Seuil, 1969.

b. Other works

Auden, W. H. Collected Shorter Poems 1927-1957. New York:
   Random House, 1966.

Blackham, H. J. Six Existentialist Thinkers. London: Routledge
   & Kegan Paul, 1952.

Freud, Sigmund. The Standard Edition of the Complete Psychological Works of Sigmund Freud, ed. by James Strachey. London: Hogarth Press, 1953-

Homans, Peter. Theology After Freud. Indianapolis: Bobbs-Merrill, 1970.

Ihde, Don. Hermeneutic Phenomenology: The Philosophy of Paul
   Ricoeur. Evanston: Northwestern University Press, 1971.

Laplanche, J. and Pontalis, J. -B. Vocabulaire de la psychanalyse.
   Paris: Presses Universitaires de France, 1968.

Preller, Victor. Divine Science and the Science of God: A Reformulation of Thomas Aquinas. Princeton, N.J.: Princeton
   University Press, 1967.

Rasmussen, David M. Mythic-Symbolic Language and Philosophical
   Anthropology: A Constructive Interpretation of the Thought
   of Paul Ricoeur. The Hague: Martinus Nijhoff, 1971.